EXPLORER'S GUIDE TO THE BIBLE

A BIG PICTURE OVERVIEW
JOHN GRAYSTON

Explorer's Guide to the Bible by John Grayston

Scripture Union, 207–209 Queensway, Bletchley, Milton Keynes, MK2 2EB, England

Email: info@scriptureunion.org.uk
www.scriptureunion.org.uk

Scripture Union USA, PO Box 987, Valley Forge, PA 19482, USA
Email: info@scriptureunion.org
www.scriptureunion.org

Scripture Union Australia, Locked Bag 2, Central Coast Business Centre, NSW 2252, Australia
www.scriptureunion.org.au

ISBN: 978 1 84427 303 4

First published in Great Britain by Scripture Union 2008

British Library Cataloguing-in-Publication Data: a catalogue record of this book is available from the British Library.

Cover design by Wild Associates Ltd.

Internal page design by Creative Pages: www.creativepages.co.uk

Printed in the UK by CPI Bookmarque, Croydon, CR0 4TD

Scripture Union is an international Christian charity working with churches in more than 130 countries providing resources to bring the good news of Jesus Christ to children, young people and families and to encourage them to develop spiritually through the Bible and prayer. As well as coordinating a network of volunteers, staff and associates who run holidays, church-based events and school Christian groups, Scripture Union produces a wide range of publications and supports those who use their resources through training programmes.

CONTENTS

How to use this book

This book does what it says on the cover! It will take you on a journey from the big picture of the Bible, zooming down to get a close-up view of each Bible book. However, at different times, you might just want a snapshot of the detail of one part of the picture. So, you could read this guidebook through at one go, or, you might choose to use the Contents page to help you pick out particular bits.

To help you get the big picture look out, too, for various illustrations, maps and explanations of some key ideas. Special Bible words are highlighted in bold and you can find out more about these in extra articles (eg 'covenant', 'kingdom') which appear at relevant points in the main text. Page numbers for these are given below so you can find them whenever these might be useful.

About the author...

John Grayston is Director of Theology for Scripture Union in England and Wales. He has been involved in Scripture Union's Bible ministry for over 30 years and is passionate about helping people to understand the Bible.

The way in...

The Bible is one of the mostly widely bought books, but perhaps one of the least read and least understood. Even if we know its stories – and increasing numbers of people, including many Christians, do not – we wonder why it is in the shape it is and what it is all about. After all, unlike any other book, it consists of a range of contributions from different authors over a period of many centuries. Its language is strange, its context alien, its relevance not immediately obvious. And yet, as Christians, we believe that this is the main way in which God speaks to us. In one sense, the main way in which God speaks to us is through Jesus – but we only know of him through the Bible.

This book is written with the conviction that Jesus is the theme of the Bible and if we want to know what God is saying through Jesus we need to know what the Bible says. It is written not with specialists in mind, but with those who want to know how the Bible fits together and what it says. My experience has been that once we get the overall picture we can begin to see what God is doing, how he is speaking and how we can know him better. This is an exciting journey – let's start exploring.

THE GLOBAL VIEW

Seeing the whole picture

Discovering Google Earth was a fascinating experience. To be able to view the whole globe and then gradually zoom in until I could identify my town, my street and finally my house gave me a whole new view on the world. As I began to visit other places I knew, I saw them too in a fresh light. I took a closer look at roads I had driven along, hills I had climbed, and the river down which I had rafted. I now understood why that bend in the road that hadn't made any sense was there. I realised why the path went south of the lake rather than north. Much of this I might have gained from a map, of course, but the principle is the same; only by seeing the whole picture can we make sense of the details.

This principle is true in many areas of life. An individual jigsaw piece makes little sense until we put it alongside others, and it is only when all are in place that we can appreciate the picture. Looking only at the anchor would hardly give much of an impression of the function of the Queen Mary – or any other large ship.

It's much the same with the Bible. We will gain a much better understanding of what the Bible is about if we stand back and take a look at the whole. Move too quickly to the detail and we may well find the passage that we are reading doesn't make a lot of sense. Worse, it may seem to make sense but we may have missed the real significance, or even misunderstood. We can read a well-known story like that of David and Goliath and see it simply as a small boy beating a giant and draw from it that size isn't important, or that power doesn't matter, or that God helps his people – all of which are true – but miss the point that this is an important part of God establishing his rule and preparing for the coming of Jesus.

We know that the Bible is a collection of books written by a range of human authors over a period of several hundred years. We are familiar with the idea of a library of different sorts of writing that make up the whole. What we sometimes fail to see is that all these different books with their varied situations and diverse characters are part of a single message from God to humanity. When the writer to the Hebrews says...

> In the past God spoke to our forefathers through the prophets at many times and in various ways, but in these last days he has spoken to us by his Son, whom he appointed heir of all things, and through whom he made the universe.
>
> *Hebrews 1:1,2*

...his point is that God has spoken in different ways and in different times but always with one purpose in mind. As we shall see, that purpose reaches its climax in Jesus.

The Bible tells a single story, the true story of God's relationship with his creation and especially with human beings. It tells us exactly how things are and explains why the world is as it is. Stories help us to make sense of our world and our lives; the story which the Bible tells makes sense of our world with its confusion, pain and brokenness. How often have we said, 'I don't understand'? Into all such situations, the Bible speaks, bringing light and hope. Don't get me wrong, I am not saying that there are always instant answers that will help us to make sense of everything that comes our way; what I am saying is that when we begin to see the world and our lives from a wider perspective we have a much greater chance of understanding. I have no detailed answer as to why my friend Liz died in her twenties, leaving a husband and a young child. Nor do I know exactly why two friends are currently struggling with redundancy and the need to relocate far from their network of friends. But what I do know is that when I see these things as part of a wider purpose, that of God's overall purpose for the world, I begin to find meaning in that which is otherwise meaningless.

So what does this big picture look like? People have described it in different ways. Vaughan Roberts in his book *God's Big Picture* (IVP) looks at the developing story of God's kingdom. NT Wright (*New Testament and the People of God*, SPCK) likens the Bible to a five-act play in which Act 1 is creation, Act 2 the fall, Act 3 the story of **Israel** and Act 4, Jesus. For him, Act 5 is still being played out in the life of the Church but we know how it will end. Chris Wright in *The Mission of God* (IVP) sees the key as being God's purpose to call all peoples back to himself in Christ. Others have used different themes to bring out the development of this story, but I want to go with what seems to me to be the most straightforward. This is a story which starts with God creating a good world, continues with human beings messing up that world, tells of how God plans to put this messed up world right in the coming of Jesus and results in a new heaven and a new earth in which everything is as God originally intended it to be.

The opening screen on Google Earth is of the entire globe. Looking at the Bible in that way, four 'continents' begin to emerge. We start with a world that God makes and proclaims good (Genesis 1:31). We can understand this when we stand before the breadth of the sea, on top of a mountain range or look at the intricate details of a flower or an insect. There is a sense of majesty and beauty and power that leaves us in awe. At times like that it's easy to see things as God intended them to be. But then we look at our TV screens and see scenes of war or disaster, or we experience some personal pain or see it in others and we realise that the world is not as it should be. Why? Because human beings decided to behave, not in the way God had intended, but in the way that they chose. So the selfish desire for power, greed and a failure to care for others mean that the world is now out of shape. We feel the effects of that. We will look at this in more detail as we press forward, but for the moment let's acknowledge that the world as we know it is not the world as God meant it to be.

The big picture

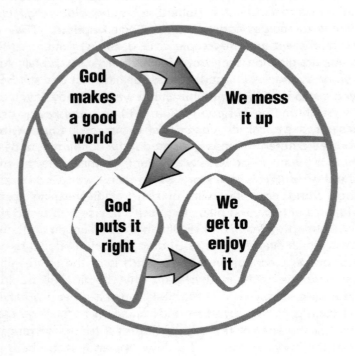

God was not, of course, taken by surprise by any of this, but it does cause him pain. In Genesis 6:6 God looks at the state of the world and we're told: 'The LORD was grieved that he had made man on the earth, and his heart was filled with pain.' Amazing as it may seem, God still loves and values the people he made; he wants to receive their praise and obedience, to enjoy the worship of the people he created. So God determines to act in a way that is staggering: he will step into the world and live as a man, showing his love and dealing with human rebellion, so that we can return to him, belong to him as his children and live as he wants. From early on in Genesis we can see God working towards this. In different ways, as we shall see, the books that Christians call the Old Testament show God working towards the point where he will act. He is preparing his people.

Then, when the time is right, God acts. He steps into human history in the person of Jesus. The Gospels tell the story, pointing again and again to the truth that, in Jesus, God is present with us. The writers major on his death because for them that is the key to it all. Jesus makes this clear:

> He said to them, 'This is what I told you while I was still with you: Everything must be fulfilled that is written about me in the Law of Moses, the Prophets and the Psalms.' Then he opened their minds so they could understand the Scriptures. He told them, 'This is what is written: The Christ will suffer and rise from the dead on the third day ...'
> Luke 24:44–46

This is a key verse. It is central to our understanding how the Bible fits together.

This is the third part of the story – God has acted and has put everything right. But it hardly looks like it. The world seems no different. That is because we wait for the final act. One scholar has likened it to the situation towards the end of the Second World War. Once the allied troops had landed on the beaches of Normandy the decisive battle had been won. But it was several months until the final victory. Another scholar uses a different picture. If we record a football match and look at it later, we may experience various highs and lows as we watch and enter into the action, even though we know that our team has already won. The result is never in doubt and cannot be changed. With Jesus' death the decisive victory over the powers of evil has been won, victory is assured and he will come back to finish it. At that point everything will be put right. The world will be as God intended. We shall enjoy peace and harmony and will experience the presence of God in a way that we find unimaginable now. Sometimes the Bible talks about this as a new heaven and a new earth (Revelation 21:1), but this doesn't mean it is plan B. Rather, this will be a full realisation of all that God had planned all along.

That's the big picture, the 'view from outer space'. It's as though we can now see how the 'continents' fit together. Which is great – but if we really want to understand the message, we shall have to look rather more closely. We need to know how the different sections contribute to our understanding of the big picture. And we need to see in more detail how they help us to understand more of what God is like and how he has worked in the world.

Along the way we need to remember that the Bible isn't given to us just to give us knowledge or even the practical wisdom that enables us to make sense of the world. In the Bible God speaks to us because he loves us – the central theme of the big story – and wants us to love him. So we read looking for a personal message of love from God. As we discover God's plan for the world we shall meet again and again a God who loves in ways that we find unimaginable, given the way that we have treated him.

There is yet more to the story, however. God is at work in the world to remake it, because of his love. He is also at work in our lives to remake us so that we can have a place in this new future that he has planned and so that we will enjoy it. The process of remaking us involves bringing us into a new relationship with him, and in changing us so that we are the sort of people he intends us to be. Here is something to look forward to.

Beautiful world

Zooming in with Google Earth, we move from the whole globe to individual continents. As we do a similar thing with the Bible and try to make more sense of the large blocks that make up the whole, the first large block we spot is creation.

The Bible starts with the momentous words, 'In the beginning God created...' (Genesis 1:1). Here is God making a world that he sees as good (Genesis 1:4,10,12,18,21,25), indeed very good when he comes to the creation of man and woman (Genesis 1:31) . Most of us will know moments when the world seems almost unbelievably beautiful. For me, such times often involve mountains; there's nothing like standing on top of a snowy peak and looking out at range after range of snow-covered mountains. Some years ago I stood in just such a position with a friend, who simply turned to me and said, 'How can anyone not believe in God?' Others will have their own favourites: the babble of a running brook, the tranquillity of a lake, the intricate detail of a flower, the wonder of a bird in flight, the splendour of a sunset... The world in which we live is a wonderful place and even people who do not believe that God created it recognise that.

The Bible says nothing about why God did it, nothing about the detailed mechanics. It simply tells that God spoke and there it was in all its beauty and wonder. There was land and sea, day and night, sun, moon and stars, mountains and lakes and rivers, elephants and ants, lambs and bumblebees, giant redwoods and tiny eyebrights hidden away in the grass of the meadow and missed by all but the most searching eyes. All of this – and so much more – coming into being at God's command.

This is where it all starts. Without it, nothing else makes sense. Omit this and it's rather like starting a novel on page 72, or starting to watch a ten-part TV series at episode four. We would have no way of making sense of the rest of the story. We don't read the creation accounts in Genesis 1 and 2 and then find that the Bible ignores creation. On the contrary, this is a theme which emerges again and again. The psalmist praises God for his world:

> He set the earth on its foundations;
>   it can never be moved.
> You covered it with the deep as with a garment;
>   the waters stood above the mountains
>
> ...
>
> How many are your works, O LORD!
>   In wisdom you made them all;
>   the earth is full of your creatures.
> *Psalm 104:5,6,24*

There's more. It isn't that God just made it all and then left it to run itself; he is still involved in all that goes on:

> These all look to you
>   to give them their food at the proper time.
> When you give it to them,
>   they gather it up;
> when you open your hand,
>   they are satisfied with good things.
> *Psalm 104:27,28*

The Bible never tells us why God made the world. God is a lover of beauty and creativity, and creates because that is his nature. The crowning point of creation, though, is this: human beings are made in order to have a relationship with God, amazing as that may seem. It appears from Genesis 3:8 that God regularly meets with Adam and Eve in the garden. When that relationship is broken, God feels pain.

Creation points us to God. Psalm 104, which we have just looked at, is a song of praise to God for what he has done. In Revelation, John has a vision of the praise in heaven – and one of the songs reflects the glory of God in creation:

> You are worthy, our Lord and God,
> > to receive glory and honour and power,
> for you created all things ...
> *Revelation 4:11*

So, as we stand back and look at the big picture, we see first of all a God who expresses himself in the creation of a beautiful world which draws attention to him and his love of beauty. Creation calls us to praise God; indeed, creation itself praises God:

> Let the sea resound, and everything in it,
> > the world, and all who live in it.
> Let the rivers clap their hands,
> > let the mountains sing together for joy;
> let them sing before the LORD,
> > for he comes to judge the earth.
> He will judge the world in righteousness
> > and the peoples with equity.
> *Psalm 98:7–9*

There is, however, another element that we have to take on board: God has given us this creation to look after (Genesis 1:28). It is entrusted to us human beings. This is a heavy responsibility. The ongoing story is largely a story of our failure to look after the world in the way that God intended.

Our theme is that the whole Bible points to Jesus. Creation is no exception. The opening words of John's Gospel talk of the Word who was made flesh – Jesus – and says:

> In the beginning was the Word, and the Word was with God, and the
> Word was God. He was with God in the beginning.
> Through him all things were made; without him nothing was made that
> has been made.
>
> *John 1:1–3*

God the Son, who comes to us as the man Jesus, was involved with Father and Spirit in the work of creation. So, already here at the very start we find Jesus.

The writer of Hebrews, speaking of Jesus, says: '... through whom he [God] made the universe' and goes on to say that the Son sustains 'all things by his powerful word' (Hebrews 1:2,3). The world as we know it is God's, and he loves it.

My wife decorates cakes. Each is a work of love, a unique creation. Each says something about her. It is the same with any artist. Each work is an expression of feeling, of desire, of hope, of fear. So it is with God's creation. In it we find God expressed. For those with eyes to see, it arouses within us a longing for something beyond, a sense that there is more than just this.

Some Christians, throughout history and still today, talk as though the world was evil and the best thing that we could do would be to escape from it. The Bible sees it very differently. It is good and God cares about it. We are to value it and live in it. It is the place where God's love for us is demonstrated and experienced in the life and work of Jesus. It is the arena in which our obedience to God is worked out and sadly, as we are about to see, it is also the sphere in which our failure and rebellion are demonstrated.

Messed up world

Reading the last chapter, you may have been feeling, 'It isn't like that. Sure, the world is beautiful, but it's also ugly. What about wars and disasters and illness and…?' And you would be right. The world is not as we would like it to be and it is not as God intended it to be. Something has gone badly wrong. We get mixed messages. While the world tells us something about its creator, it also sends out messages that confuse and depress.

As we take in the big picture, the next key point is in Genesis 3. Here we find the first man and woman enjoying the world which God made and living in harmony with their environment, with one another and with God. It is a great picture, summing up all that is good about the world. But into this picture of harmony and well-being, a shadow falls. The symphony is interrupted by a discordant note.

God has not asked much. He has given them everything to enjoy. Food aplenty, enticing fruit – it's all theirs. One thing, and only one, is off-limits. For a time all is well and then comes the voice of the tempter – 'Why not?' The suggestion is that God has only forbidden this fruit because it will give them God-like powers and he wants to keep this for himself. Suddenly there are new possibilities. Perhaps, all along, God was conning them. Perhaps they can have new powers, new authority. They can have access to knowledge they have only previously dreamt of. The thought grows until it becomes irresistible. The fruit is taken and life will never be the same again. For in that action all has changed.

Popular thinking doesn't get beyond the eating of a piece of fruit, often mistakenly referred to as an apple, which is possibly a bit tough on Granny Smith! The real problem is not in eating the fruit but in the arrogant determination to be independent. Here, Adam and Eve are saying to God, 'We don't need you. We can manage on our own. We can run our lives better than you can.' This was the heart of **sin** then, and is the heart of sin now. That first act in the garden is massively significant; it is a one-off that changed the world for ever – not just the lives of humans, but the whole of creation. But the same act of independence and rejection is also played out day after day. Just like Adam and Eve, we think that we can do better on our own. We have grown up; we no longer need the prop of religion. Faith is a psychological crutch for the weak. We have all heard the arguments, put so strongly by Henley in his poem 'Invictus':

I am the master of my fate;
I am the captain of my soul.

Adam couldn't have put it better. But what a fate! Adam and Eve find themselves excluded from the garden; they no longer have access to the source of life, symbolised by another tree, but to be found in God alone. Excluded they now find that the world, previously such a source of pleasure, is now a source of pain. Work which had been a source of satisfaction is now just a chore. The natural elements, formerly cooperative, are now sometimes hostile. The consequences of not doing things God's way are massive and far-reaching.

Sin

Talk to most people about sin and they think of sins – murder, adultery (if it still features in the list), theft – but these are only the outworking of the deeper sin, the rejection of God. The Bible has many terms for sin. The most common in the Old Testament suggests 'missing the mark' or 'falling short'. Another suggests something that is bent or out of shape.

Others emphasise the idea of rebellion or ungodliness.

In the New Testament, the most common word also carries the meaning of missing the mark and other terms carry similar meanings to those in the Old Testament: lawlessness, ungodliness, falling short, disobedience.

Sin, while it has consequences in our relationships with one another, is always something directed against God. It brings with it guilt – a word which implies we have amassed a debt which has to be paid off. Because sin is an affront to all that God is, it damages our relationship with him. Only when our sin is forgiven and our debt written off can that relationship be restored.

This is why we experience the world as it is – both as the beautiful creation of a creative God and as the messed up, broken thing we live and struggle in. When I was a child, London's Science Museum was a favourite and one feature I particularly enjoyed was a large-scale, walk-in model of a coal mine. Imagine my disappointment on one visit when I found a large notice on the entrance saying, 'Out of order'. We will all have similar frustrating experiences: the lift in the tower block, the cash machine, the one ride we really wanted to go on in the theme park. This world has an 'Out of order' notice on it. It's rather like my last computer towards the end of its life, when unpredictable things would happen – blue screens, sudden crashes, refusals to save and ominous memory failures. The world is like that.

Human hatred and wars, natural disasters, illness, death, broken relationships – all stem from the original decision of Adam and Eve to go their own way rather than God's, a decision which is repeated generation after generation. The damage has been done and however we might long for it, it is too late, there is no way back to the garden. We long for something better. The optimists tell us that things are improving, that we are more civilised than our ancestors – but there is little evidence for it. The last 100 years have seen more bloodshed than any other time in history. The dream of a world getting better died for many in the trenches of the Somme and, for others, in the huts of Auschwitz, Stalin's Gulag, the killing fields of Cambodia, or in so many other expressions of human greed, selfishness and cruelty. This is not to say that humans are not capable of amazing acts of kindness and generosity. Just like the rest of creation, we send out mixed messages. We are a bundle of contradictions. Made in God's image we still bear his likeness, but it is obscured by our rebellion and determination to go our own way.

Being away from the garden means that we are away from God. We are all in the situation of the Lost Son (Luke 15:11–32) – away from home. It is possible, as he finds, to hide the sense of alienation and purposelessness, but sooner or later it catches up with most of us. Augustine, Bishop of Hippo in North Africa in the fifth century, put it this way: 'You have made us for yourself and our hearts are restless until they find their rest in you.' There has to be something better, both for the world and for us. We, if we are remotely sensitive, cry out: 'Why are things the way they are? When will they change? Where is God?'

Putting it right

We have taken a look at two 'continents' and are only in Genesis chapter 3! This need not worry us – we have already seen that the themes which first emerge there are to be found throughout the Bible. Our next 'continent' takes up rather more space.

We ended the last chapter with the cry which comes from the heart of every sensitive person. Thankfully, that struggle with the way things are is not the end of the story. Even as things begin to fall apart there are the first stirrings of hope. As God points out to Adam and Eve the consequences of their action and rebukes the tempter, he suggests that one day the effects of their action will be reversed:

> And I will put enmity
>> between you and the woman,
>> and between your offspring and hers;
> he will crush your head,
>> and you will strike his heel.
>
> *Genesis 3:15*

Not much, admittedly, but a clear hint of what is to come. When God then provides clothing for Adam and Eve (who have suddenly become aware of their nakedness), he shows at the very least that he still cares about their welfare. Some have seen in this another hint of the way in which the effect of human rebellion would be dealt with through **sacrifice**.

Timeline: creation to eternity

Creation and Eve rebel
the flood

Adam and Noah

Abraham called
Escape from Egypt

Settlement of the Promised Land

King David
Kingdom splits – northern kingdom

Fall of Samaria – end of Isaiah Jeremiah

Exile in Babylon

Jesus' life, death and resurrection

Jesus comes back, new heaven and earth

1600   1200   800   400   200   0

When we zoom in and look more closely at the details of Genesis, we will see more of the effects of human rebellion and selfishness. We will also see that God is working on a way to deal with it. He has not been caught by surprise – he has known that this would happen and, before he even made the world, he knew what he would do. He plans to save the world:

> ... with the precious blood of Christ, a lamb without blemish or defect. He was chosen before the creation of the world, but was revealed in these last times for your sake.
>
> *1 Peter 1:19,20*

Before the world exists God plans what what he will do in the face of human sin. (see timeline on opposite page)

In our 'outer space' view of the Bible this is far and away the biggest 'continent'. In terms of the layout of the Bible it takes up the rest of the Old Testament and the bulk of the New. There are centuries of preparation when people live with the promise which is fulfilled when Jesus comes. This promise is repeated again and again. One of its earliest and clearest expressions is God's promise to Abraham (at the time, called Abram), a promise not just for himself but for the whole world:

> I will make you into a great nation
> > and I will bless you;
> I will make your name great,
> > and you will be a blessing.
> I will bless those who bless you,
> > and whoever curses you I will curse;
> and all peoples on earth
> > will be blessed through you.
>
> *Genesis 12:2,3*

Abraham would not have understood all that this meant but he takes it at face value and trusts God. With hindsight we can see that, as we travel through the Old Testament, this promise is renewed again and again. Against the backdrop of human failure, there are times when it seems this might mess everything up, but God always comes through, his purposes will always be fulfilled.

When Abraham's great-grandson, Joseph, ends up in Egypt and then finally the whole clan are enslaved, it seems impossible. Enter Moses, God's man for the moment, who leads the Israelites out of Egypt. The sea parts, the Egyptian army is destroyed, God saves and delivers his people. Moses' successor, Joshua, leads the people into the land which God had promised to Abraham and all seems well. But human failure raises its head again and the people assert their independence. The Lord, who had brought them out of Egypt, who had made them into a people, who had entered into a special agreement with them, is put on one side and replaced by the local gods, whom they think will be better at ensuring a good harvest. Nor do these local gods make the same moral demands; indeed, worship involving fertility rites and sex in the sanctuary has a certain attraction.

At no point does God give up. In the early days in the new land, there are repeated cycles of rebellion, which lead to God giving them over to their enemies, at which point they turn back to him and he sends leaders to deliver them. These leaders are known as judges, and are a combination of political, military and spiritual leaders. The last one, Samuel, gives way to the first king, Saul. There is then a succession of kings – some are true to God, many are not. There are prophets who call the people back to God: men like Elijah, Isaiah, Amos and Hosea who remind the people of their responsibilities towards the Lord and one another. As things slide from bad to worse, the kingdom divides into two, and within 300 years of their arrival in the Promised Land, the northern kingdom, known as **Israel**, with its capital in Samaria, has fallen to the Assyrians and disappears.

Meanwhile the southern kingdom, Judah, staggers on, but continues to move away from God until the people are taken into exile by the Babylonians. However, throughout this period, a new hope emerges. Originally the hope had been that the king would ensure that God was worshipped and the nation ruled justly. As that hope dwindles, the prophets begin to look forward to a time when God would send a new king, the **Messiah**, who would rule for him. Isaiah puts it like this:

The Spirit of the Sovereign LORD is on me,
　　because the LORD has anointed me
　　to preach good news to the poor.
He has sent me to bind up the broken-hearted,
　　to proclaim freedom for the captives
　　and release from darkness for the prisoners,
　to proclaim the year of the LORD's favour
　　and the day of vengeance of our God,
to comfort all who mourn ...
Isaiah 61:1,2

Messiah

We are familiar with the term 'Messiah' but perhaps even more with the term 'Christ'. We often talk about Jesus Christ as though this was his surname, but nothing could be further from the truth. The Hebrew word 'Messiah' and the Greek word 'Christ' both mean anointed. In the Old Testament, people were anointed to indicate that they had been called to a special office. Kings (1 Samuel 10:1; 16:1–3,12,13), priests (Exodus 30:30) and prophets (1 Kings 19:16) were anointed. This involved pouring oil over them as a mark that they were called and were now dedicated to the role. Even the furniture in the tabernacle was anointed to show that it was special to God (Exodus 30:25–29).

In time, with the failure of the kings and the priests to be what God had called them to be, an expectation arose that God would send a king who would rule for him. By the time of Jesus, expectations of a Messiah were very strong. For most people, this meant a great leader who would fight against the Romans (who were by then occupying the country) and who would throw them out. But Jesus has to explain that the role of Messiah, as God had planned it, was very different. It was to be one who would save the world from sin. Far from being a great military or political leader, he would be the humble, suffering servant of whom Isaiah speaks (Isaiah 52:13 – 53:12). Jesus was called and sent by God and, whenever we refer to him as Christ, we are reminding ourselves of that.

Jesus sees his ministry in these terms and quotes these words early on in his public ministry (Luke 4:18,19).

The prophet Jeremiah sees more explicitly that something will have to take place which can change people from the inside out. The idea that we can do what God requires in our own strength does not stand up. God will have to do something new:

> 'This is the covenant that I will make with the house of Israel
>   after that time,' declares the LORD.
> 'I will put my law in their minds
>   and write it on their hearts.
> I will be their God,
>   and they will be my people.
> No longer will a man teach his neighbour,
>   or a man his brother, saying, "Know the LORD,"
> because they will all know me,
>   from the least of them to the greatest ...'
> Jeremiah 31:33,34

Jeremiah's key point is that a time will come when our motivation for obeying God will be something that comes from within – changed people, rather than something which is imposed from outside – a set of regulations.

The return from exile kindled brief hopes, but these soon died. The Old Testament gives way to a long period of silence lasting nearly 400 years. There is a brief period of independence but, for the most part, the people of God are under the control of foreign powers – Babylon, Persia, Greece and, finally, Rome.

Looking at this picture we might wonder what God was doing. Throughout this long turbulent history, marked by human rebellion and self-centredness, there have always been those who have remained true to God and in whom he was at work. This is a time of preparation and promise, but fulfilment will come.

Then in the fullness of time, God acts. An angel comes to a teenage girl and announces that although she is not married, she will have a son. This is the fulfilment of the age-old promise originally given to Abraham. It is through him that the nations will be blessed. This is the long looked-for king, the awaited **Messiah**. The first four books of the New Testament, the Gospels, tell the story of his life, recording his actions, his teaching (much of it in the form of stories), and his death. In one sense these are biographies, but they are very strange biographies. Over one third of each is given to the last week of Jesus' life. The first 30 years are, with the exception of the accounts of his birth in Matthew and Luke, completely ignored. This should alert us to something that we will explore in more detail later; the death of Jesus is somehow as important to these writers as his life. We know, of course, that his death is not 'the end', for each of these Gospels closes by telling us that he rose from the dead.

This is the heart of the whole Bible story. It is the event which makes sense of all that went before and all that comes after. God has broken in and life will never be the same again. Just as the first act of rebellion messed up the world and all that goes on in it, so the death and resurrection of Jesus puts everything right. All that went wrong then is now reversed; the car that was sliding down the hill out of control is now halted and set back on course. This is achieved through Jesus' life of obedience which reverses the act of disobedience, and through his death in which he takes onto himself the penalty for human rebellion.

The rest of the New Testament tells the story of the change which results. The **good news** of what God has done spreads out from Jerusalem and, by the time we arrive at the end of Acts, it has reached Rome, the centre of the empire which then controlled the world. By this time, too, most of the letters that make up much of the rest of the New Testament have been written. Here we see the early Christians thinking under the inspiration of the Spirit about the significance of Jesus' life, death and resurrection. Between them, they explain the significance of the story which the Gospels tell. They help us to understand that Jesus died so that we could live. They show how his life and death fit in with the Old Testament background. They call us to respond.

They also help us to work out what it means to live as followers of Jesus in the world. Their society may have been very different to ours, but it was no easier to be a Christian. We see them struggling, as we do, with temptation and moral failure. They fall out with one another, just as we do today. They face opposition, often so fierce that they die for their **faith**. They are misunderstood. Through all of this, they keep believing that Jesus has given them something new, that he has brought them into a new relationship with God and that they are the start of something bigger and better than they could fully understand. They experience the power of the Holy Spirit at work in them in new ways and believe that he is creating a new community. They know that just as Jesus has been raised from the dead, so his followers will be raised. So they look forward with hope, beyond the pain and suffering, to a new world where all will be as God intends it to be.

This is all very well, but if Jesus has, in reality, done something that is new and earth-and-heaven renewing, why do we see so little of it here and now? That is a question that the early Christians would have known and understood, despite their clear and certain hope for the future. It is to that, the last of our four 'continents', we now turn.

Secure future

A world out of order, but repaired – so what's the problem? Why are things not running perfectly now? For the answer we have to look into the future. With the life, death and resurrection of Jesus, everything changed, but we don't yet see all the effects. Jesus is King, but his rule is not yet universally recognised. One day it will be:

> ... at the name of Jesus every knee should bow,
> in heaven and on earth and under the earth,
> and every tongue confess that Jesus Christ is Lord,
> to the glory of God the Father.
>
> *Philippians 2:10,11*

Jesus promises that he will come back again. He knows that what he has done is decisive. When he says from the cross, 'It is finished' (John 19:30), it doesn't mean that his life is over but that his work has been completed. But he teaches his followers that they will not see the full effects of this until he returns. In John 14:1–3 he promises that he will come back and his followers will then be with him for ever. Mark 13 is not an easy chapter to understand, but it seems to point to a time when 'the Son of Man' (a term with its roots in Daniel 7:13 and which Jesus uses to describe himself) will return and will finally destroy evil. Matthew 25 contains several parables warning Jesus' followers to be ready when he comes back.

We are not the first to wonder why this has all taken so long. Even in the first century, Christians had to face the charge that Jesus had failed to keep his promise. Peter responds like this:

> With the Lord a day is like a thousand years, and a thousand years are like a day. The Lord is not slow in keeping his promise, as some understand slowness. He is patient with you, not wanting anyone to perish, but everyone to come to repentance.
>
> *2 Peter 3:8,9*

God holds off for one reason only: so that more people might put their **faith** in Jesus and enter into eternal life.

Others put forward the idea that Jesus had already come back in a 'spiritual sense'. This does not really tie in with what Jesus actually said. Paul has to deal with the same idea in his letter to his young helper, Timothy:

> … Among them are Hymenaeus and Philetus, who have wandered away from the truth. They say that the resurrection has already taken place, and they destroy the faith of some.
>
> *2 Timothy 2:17,18*

Some people still believe something similar. The idea is as wrong now as it was then.

Whenever Jesus' return is mentioned in the New Testament, it is always something which is going to occur in the future. In 1 Thessalonians 4:16 Paul says, 'For the Lord himself will come down from heaven,' and goes on to point out that when he does, we will all go to be with him for ever. This is the **good news**. Hebrews 9:28 says that Jesus will come a second time to bring salvation to all those who are waiting for him, but in the verse before hints that there will also be judgement. Paul spells this out:

> For we must all appear before the judgment seat of Christ, that each
> one may receive what is due to him for the things done while in the
> body, whether good or bad.
>
> *2 Corinthians 5:10*

There is more to the return of Jesus than simply a nice reunion – or the thought of having to give account for ourselves. There is a much bigger dimension that is too often missed. When Jesus comes back we shall move into a totally new era – there will be a new heaven and a new earth (2 Peter 3:13). The world as we experience it now will be rolled up like an old, unwanted shirt and thrown onto the fire; the new will emerge, but it will not be completely different. It *will* be all that God intended the original to be.

The last book in the Bible, Revelation, is not an easy read. We shall look at it in more detail later. For the moment, it's worth noticing that it's written in a special style which the first readers would have recognised, using picture language and a great deal of imagery which looks very strange to us. It was originally written to a group of churches in the area we now know as Turkey. They were being persecuted for their faith and the letter is designed to encourage them to keep going. The central theme is that God is in control of the whole of human history and that a day is coming when he will put all things right. Again, we find the vision of a new heaven and earth. God will live with his people in a new way. He will be their comfort. Evil, oppression and injustice will be wiped out. The last chapter of the Bible ends as it began – in a garden. There is a river; there are trees; but now the leaves of the tree are for healing. It is specifically stated that there is no more curse. The effects of that first act of human rebellion and independence are now reversed. Harmony has been restored – between God and creation, between God and men and women, between humanity and the natural creation. Over 800 years before John received the vision of renewed creation, Isaiah had seen it coming:

The wolf will live with the lamb,
> the leopard will lie down with the goat,
the calf and the lion and the yearling together;
> and a little child will lead them.
The cow will feed with the bear,
> their young will lie down together,
> and the lion will eat straw like the ox.
The infant will play near the hole of the cobra,
> and the young child put his hand into the viper's nest.
They will neither harm nor destroy
> on all my holy mountain,
for the earth will be full of the knowledge of the LORD
> as the waters cover the sea.

Isaiah 11:6–9

From the moment when things went wrong, God has been working towards this point. History is not some endless cycle going round in circles, nor is it the story of gradual human progress, as a quick glance at the history of the twentieth and early twenty-first centuries will show, nor is it a pointless game in which we all have to make the best we can of it; no, it is headed in a direction determined by God towards a new world in which he will be worshipped as he deserves. This is the destination to which everything has been pointing since Genesis 3. And it has been brought about through Jesus.

We have now sketched out the broad shape of the landscape. We can see how the various parts fit together to form one connected whole. We can also see that, while it is helpful to think in terms of a map or a globe as we see the Bible as it is laid out in front of us, this way of looking at it does not tell us everything. For the Bible tells a story that progresses. It is also like a drama unfolding before our eyes. Perhaps to get the best understanding, we need both models. The map helps us to see how the various parts fit together; the drama tells us how God has been at work throughout history.

THE CONTINENTAL VIEW

A closer look

With our Google Earth view of the world, when we start to move in closer, we notice that the terrain is very varied. There are hills and mountains, lakes and rivers, valleys and forests; each with its own special features and attractions. Each requires a different sort of navigation – a gentle stroll beside the river requires different preparation, different skills and a different degree of fitness to a long mountain hike. Each gives a different sort of pleasure. Each moves us in a different way.

The Bible is like this once we start to get in closer. There are different sorts of writing, different authors, different situations. The rest of this section will be about looking at larger blocks of material, which on our model are a bit like countries, but first it is worth thinking about the nature of the terrain. Just as we need to understand something about the nature of the land if we are to get the best out of it and avoid the dangers of getting lost, falling over the edge of a cliff or finding ourselves, literally, up the creek without a paddle, so we need to know something of the nature of the parts of the Bible that we are looking at. So let's take a brief look. For those who want more detail, check out the list of books for further reading on page 127.

The contents of the Bible

How did we come to have the books that we have in the Bible? The Old Testament was largely agreed by the time of Jesus. The Hebrew scriptures are arranged differently to the Christian Old Testament, but the contents are the same. There is common agreement that the 39 books that we find in the Old Testament are inspired by God in a special way. In 2 Timothy 3:16 Paul talks about the Scripture as being 'God-breathed', meaning that in some way it has its origin in God. Peter writes: 'For prophecy never had its origin in the will of man, but men spoke from God as they were carried along by the Holy Spirit' (2 Peter 1:21).

When it came to deciding which books have authority in the early Church, the determining factor was whether or not they originated with the apostles. By the middle of the second century, the list was pretty much agreed along the lines of the New Testament as we know it. There were a few books that were still debated, but most of the questions had been agreed by the middle of the fourth century.

From time to time there are arguments that other books should be included. The Da Vinci Code popularised the idea that books like the Gospel of Thomas or the Gospel of Mary Magdalene preserve older and better traditions than the Gospels we have. The arguments are complicated, but it is generally agreed that these are much later and lack the quality of those that the Church under the guidance of the Spirit has accepted as inspired.

Here's how the books are arranged in the Hebrew Bible.

Law (*Torah*): Genesis to Deuternomy.

Prophets (*Nebi'im*) Former: Joshua, Judges, 1 and 2 Samuel, 1 and 2 Kings.

Latter: Isaiah, Jeremiah, Ezekiel, Hosea, Joel, Amos, Obadiah, Jonah. Micah, Nahum, Habakkuk, Zephaniah, Haggai, Zechariah, Malachi. The last twelve, whom Christians term 'the minor prophets' on the basis of length, are sometimes referred to in the Hebrew Bible as 'The Book of the Twelve'.

Writings: Psalms, Proverbs, Job, Song of Songs, Ruth, Lamentations, Ecclesiastes, Esther, Daniel, Ezra, Nehemiah, 1 and 2 Chronicles.

Law

The books of law show us what this life of obedience looks like for God's people as they live together and as they demonstrate that they are his. As we have already seen, God's aim is to bless the nations – and the boundaries which law supplies in society are one of the ways in which he does that. Most of the laws are found in the books of Exodus, Leviticus and Deuteronomy, although the first five books of the Bible are often spoken of as the Law. They contain rules about worship, about life in society – defining crimes, describing the way that people can best live together and encouraging care for the poor and the weak, about family life and sexual behaviour. It seems that the people cannot keep the Law in the way that God asks, so a different way must be found. And it is built into the structure of the law itself. In the worship of the tabernacle and temple and in the sacrificial system, we have pointers to Jesus. Not all the laws will apply to us in exactly the way that they did then, but they do provide timeless values and priorities for living in society.

History

Much of the Old Testament is taken up with history. We read the early stories of Abraham, of Joseph and then of the Israelites leaving Egypt and entering the land that God had promised to give them. Then there is the history of their time in the land. History tells us how God was at work at the time – and, by telling us what sort of God he is and how he relates to people, helps us to see how he might relate to us. Although the stories of those we read about are not our stories, we will often find that we can enter their stories because ours are so similar. We share a common humanity, despite the different circumstances in which we live. We share emotions, we live in relationship with others, we struggle with disappointment and failure.

The books that run from Joshua to Esther in most English Bibles are normally called the history books (see p52), but there is also history in other books – Genesis, Exodus and Numbers, along with some of the prophets, especially Jeremiah and Isaiah chapters 36–39.

The story of the Old Testament

EGYPT

R Nile

SINAI

Red Sea

The Great Sea (Mediterranean Sea)

Tarsus

CANAAN

Sidon
Tyre
Damascus

Shechem
Bethel
Jerusalem
Hebron
Beersheba

Haran

R Euphrates

R Tigris

Babylon

Ur

Jacob's family moves to Egypt c1700 BC

Moses leads Israelites to Promised Land c1280 BC

Exile to Babylon c597–587 BC

Return of exiles to Jerusalem c538 BC

Abraham travels to Canaan c2000–1900 BC

0   100   200   300   400 Kms
0   100   200   Miles

Above all, we can see in this history that God is working towards a purpose. As we have seen, from the point where man and woman decided to go their own way and ignore God, God is working to bring about a new relationship which he eventually does in Jesus. In the Hebrew scriptures, the books that we call history are termed the Former Prophets. So when Jesus opened the Scriptures to the disciples on the road to Emmaus (Luke 24:27), he included the history books in his explanation. These books tell the story of God's people, sometimes as they serve him and sometimes as they choose to go their own way. What they demonstrate is that unless God intervenes, there is not much that we can do to sort out the problem.

Prophets

The prophets, whose writings take up the last section of the Old Testament, running from Isaiah to Malachi, address this situation, initially calling the people back to God, and reminding them of the consequences of their failure. They also begin to speak of a future in which God will be with his people in a new way and will enable them to live as he wants. We think of prophecy as something which looks at the future and, while the Old Testament prophets do that, this is not their main function. Their primary purpose is to explain what God is doing in the world and to call the people back to a life of obedience to him. Much of the future they look forward to has been fulfilled in Jesus; some has yet to be fulfilled. Their repeated calls to live in obedience have as much force in our own world as they did then.

Wisdom

The Old Testament also contains what are called the wisdom books. These are varied and include books like Job and Ecclesiastes which wrestle with some of the big problems of life, and Proverbs which majors on sound and pithy advice about living sensibly. Many of the nations around **Israel** had their own form of wisdom writings. The distinctive thing about Israel's wisdom is the way in which it ultimately points to the fear of the Lord as the beginning of wisdom (Proverbs 9:10).

Psalms

Psalms is in a category of its own. Originally, they were individual poems and songs agonising over national and personal tragedies, celebrating the glory of God in creation and history, praising the power of God to save his people, regretting personal and national failure. Later, they came to form a collection of songs which took their place in the people's worship of God. Hebrew poetry is not quite the same as modern western poetry. It shares a use of strong, vivid images and sometimes the use of rhythm, but it also often uses phrases in parallel to build an idea. To us this may look a little like repetition. Psalms are not the only books to be written in poetic form – much of the prophets' material takes the form of poetry too and therefore uses powerful images and descriptive language to touch the emotions as well as the mind. Often they help us to form our own responses to God.

Gospels and Acts

When we turn to the New Testament, we find more historical material in the Gospels and in Acts. The Gospels are, in effect, a sort of biography, but they do not read like any biography that we know. They all give the bulk of their attention to the last week of Jesus' life, not because the writers thought that the rest of his life and ministry was not important, but because they knew that it was in Jesus' death and resurrection that God acted decisively to bring about the salvation of the world. Within the Gospels are different forms of writing: accounts of Jesus' actions, and summaries of his teaching, some of it in the form of parables. There are stories of healings and of conflict, stories which demonstrate the power and authority of Jesus and stories which reveal the opposition of the authorities and the slowness of his disciples to understand who he is and why he had come.

Acts is the continuation of Luke's Gospel. In it, he tells the story of the spread of the **good news** after Jesus has returned to heaven. While he does record sermons, most of it is historical narrative – some of it apparently written from Luke's own eyewitness experience and all with skill and attention to detail. Acts is not designed to give us a blueprint for the way we should 'do church' today; rather, it tells us how God moved things forward at that time. But if we look at the way God acted then, it will help us to understand how he might be at work today, and where we might discover him.

Letters

The rest of the New Testament consists of letters – even the strange book of Revelation is really a letter. Most are written to individual churches, some to groups of churches and some to individuals. They deal with local situations, many peculiar to the culture and attitudes of the time. In the light of this, they reflect on what we are to make of the death and resurrection of Jesus, and how we are to live in the light of what God has done in and through him. As they do this they outline the central convictions that Christians have held to over the ages. Often it will be like listening to one side of a telephone conversation and trying to fill in the gaps. Applying the practical instruction will need care – we need to think about the local situation and the reasons behind the instruction, and ask how it might apply in our very different settings.

Bible books – law

Genesis 1,2	Creation.
Genesis 3–11	Steady decline as humanity rejects God.
Genesis 12–36	God's promise; Abraham, Isaac and Jacob.
Genesis 37–50	Joseph, Abraham's descendants in Egypt.
Exodus 1–19	God delivers Abraham's descendants from Egypt.
Exodus 20–40	Rules for living and worshipping.
Leviticus	Rules for living and worshipping.
Numbers	More rules, some history and lots of lists.
Deuteronomy	Even more rules – and Moses encourages the people to keep on serving God.

Rules, rules, rules

The very idea of rules divides us – some of us love them; most of us regard them as necessary, if slightly annoying; others do all they can to find ways around them, or ignore them. Other than convinced anarchists, however, we recognise that without them, society could not function. If there were no rules about which side of the road to drive on there would be chaos.

The first five books of the Bible are generally termed 'books of the Law', but there is far more to them than that. There are rules, important rules, which show how God's people are meant to live, but first we need to get the broader picture. Let's try breaking down the content of these books so we can explore them. Take a look at the table opposite.

So, yes, there are rules but they are set in the story of God choosing and making a people who will serve him. The story starts with themes we have already met: the beauty of creation and Adam and Eve determined to assert their independence. By the end of Genesis 3, the scene is set. Human beings, determined to go their own way, are out of relationship with God. The story gets steadily worse. Genesis 4–11 tells a story of unmitigated failure. Society collapses, violence breaks out, things get so bad that God regrets that he has made the world (Genesis 6:6) – and destroys it with a flood. But not totally.

One man, Noah, along with his family, is spared in the ark. Not only is this about preserving creation, it is a picture of what God will later do to save all. Alongside the promise never to destroy the world in such a way again is the indication that God is in the business of putting right this sad and broken world (Genesis 8:20–22). As we have seen and will see again, God loves it and is determined that all will be well with it. These chapters culminate in another great human act of arrogance and disobedience – the attempt to build the tower of Babel (Genesis 11:1–9): arrogance in the attempt to take God's role; disobedience in refusing to obey his command to populate the whole world.

At this point the staggering plan emerges. God takes an old man and his childless wife in an obscure part of the Middle East – somewhere in what is now southern Iraq – and announces that through their descendants he will bless the nations of the world (Genesis 12:1–3). As plans go, this is not overly convincing. The casual onlooker might have been forgiven for raised eyebrows or a quiet laugh. Indeed, that is precisely what Abraham and Sarah did. But whatever their, and our, doubts and questions might be, this is how God is going to do it. There can be little doubt in anyone's mind that this will be God's solution and not a human one. For human ones have failed and will fail again. From now on, a course of actions has been set in motion that will change the world for the better. It will take centuries to work through, but work through it will.

The story moves on through Isaac and Jacob and then Joseph. Often it seems that the whole plan is in danger of falling apart, but God continues to keep it on track. Even when Joseph is sold into slavery in Egypt and his brothers look as if they will starve to death, God, according to Joseph, is still in control.

> You intended to harm me, but God intended it for good to accomplish
> what is now being done, the saving of many lives.
> Genesis 50:20

God is still in control 400 years later when a new pharaoh (or king) comes to the throne and oppresses the Israelites, making them slaves. Again it seems that the promise might come to nothing. Who should God bring to the rescue but a murderer on the run, looking after sheep in the desert! What does he do with this unlikely character, who confesses to have no speaking skills (Exodus 3:1 – 4:17)? Moses is sent off to speak to the king of Egypt, the powerful oppressive ruler. And so to the plagues and to the escape from Egypt which we call the Exodus. The plagues demonstrate the supreme power of God against the gods of Egypt. The escape proves his ability to save his people. The most significant thing here is not the parting of the waters, magnificent though that is as a demonstration of God's saving power. No, the most significant thing is the **sacrifice** of the Passover lamb which points forward to what God is going to do in Jesus. The escape shows us what God can do and defines how he is going to do it.

Israel

The language used in the Bible can be confusing! The nation of Israel has its origins in the sons of Jacob, who is also called 'Israel' (Genesis 35:10). Their descendants end up in slavery in Egypt and are delivered by God. At this time – and later – they are sometimes referred to as Hebrews, a term first used to describe Abraham in Genesis 14:13, thus indicating that they are descendants of Abraham. The people are also described as sons or children of Israel or Israelites. When they settle in the land of Canaan ('the Promised Land') they are often referred to by the names of their individual tribes, each going back to the sons of Jacob. After the kingdom splits, the north keeps the name Israel while the south is called Judah. By New Testament times, the northern kingdom has long since disappeared and the term Israelite can be applied to anyone who is ethnically from the line of Jacob. The term 'Jew' or 'Jewish' covers the same ground and derives from Judah. The letter to the Hebrews was written to Jews who had become Christians.

For centuries, **Israel** looked back on the escape from Egypt as God's supreme saving act. The writers of the psalms and the prophets speak of the escape from Egypt when they want to remind Israel of what God has done. In the New Testament it is seen as a picture of what God has done in Jesus. In Luke 9:31, as Jesus talks with Moses and Elijah at his transfiguration he uses the Greek word exodus ('departure', NIV) which could hardly have failed to recall to the first readers of the Gospel the Old Testament story. And Paul talks of Jesus as 'our Passover lamb' (1 Corinthians 5:7). All this shows us how the Old Testament points to Jesus.

The next event is key in taking a bunch of slaves and forming them into a nation, shaping their identity as the people of God. They come to Mount Sinai and God gives them the Ten Commandments. This is where we first encounter the rules. What we often fail to notice is the context in which these are given. **Israel** comes to the mountain and before there is any mention of rules, God tells them how much he cares for them and reminds them of what he has done for them. So, the Ten Commandments are given in the context of a special relationship. The word **'covenant'** is used to describe this. The rules are not a harsh imposition but an expression of mutual love. They are not given to grind people down but to show them how to live in ways that will bring peace to their relationships with God and with one another. Far from being, as we often see them, a mark of oppression, they are a demonstration of love and grace, of his desire that people live fulfilled and happy lives.

Covenant

Covenant is an important idea that crops up again and again in the Bible. Many scholars believe that this is the key theme that holds the Bible together. A covenant is a solemn and binding agreement between two individuals or groups, one of whom may be greater than the other. God makes a covenant with Noah (Genesis 9:8–11) promising never to destroy the earth again. God enters into a covenant with Abraham (Genesis 17:1–14, but with roots in Genesis 12:1–3). This covenant forms the basis of his plan to save the world and is renewed when he takes the Israelites out of Egypt and brings them to Sinai (Exodus 19:1–6). All the laws are an expression of **Israel**'s part in the covenant. God will love them, protect them and care for them, but only if they are obedient to him. There are many parallels between Deuteronomy and ancient covenant agreements which have been found; we can see Deuteronomy as spelling out the nature of the covenant between God and his people. This covenant is renewed with the promise to David (Psalm 89:3,4; see 2 Samuel 7:1–16).

The prophets constantly have to remind the people of their covenant responsibilities and Jeremiah points out that the covenant can be broken and that God will not be bound by it if the people disobey.

> This is what the LORD says: 'If you can break my covenant with the day and my covenant with the night, so that day and night no longer come at their appointed time, then my covenant with David my servant – and my covenant with the Levites who are priests ministering before me – can be broken and David will no longer have a descendant to reign on his throne.'
>
> *Jeremiah 33:20,21*

Jeremiah also looks forward to a time when God will make a new covenant which will not require the people to obey an external law but will give them a new inner motivation to love and obey him, to live their lives to please him (Jeremiah 31:31–34). When Jesus shared the Passover meal with his disciples he spoke of the blood of the new covenant which he was making (Luke 22:20). The reason for the mention of blood is because the covenant at Sinai was ratified by **sacrifice**. God now has a new agreement which binds us to him and him to us, but this also requires our obedience. Later New Testament writers also pick up this idea of the covenant between God and his people which he has made in Jesus. All the Old Testament statements about covenant focus on what Jesus would later do.

Much of the rest of Exodus and the whole of Leviticus are taken up with detailed rules. Many of these are about how and where

God's people were to worship – detailed instructions for the appointment of priests, for the building of the special tent for worship and for the sacrifices that would be a central part of that worship. There are instructions for special feast days. Much of this seems very strange to us, but it reminds us that God is a holy God to be approached with care, that our sin and rebellion separate us from him, but that he has made a way for us to be forgiven and restored, and that this involves costly **sacrifice**. In the New Testament, the book of Hebrews explains how all of this points forward to Jesus.

Numbers sees **Israel** coming to the edge of the Promised Land where they send in twelve spies. The report is encouraging; the land is all that they could ask. Only one problem – it is already occupied by some rather large people who live in well-fortified cities. We might think that this would not be a problem to the God who had recently defeated Egypt, the dominant superpower, compared with whom the inhabitants of Canaan are completely insignificant. Two of the spies have the faith to see this, but for the people, this is a bridge too far. They complain, and as a result end up wandering in the wilderness for another 40 years. The rest of Numbers gives a lot of detail about the people and their tribes. This is real history with real people; it is here, in this world as we know it, that God works out his plans. And it is through these people, these descendants of Abraham who fail so often and so spectacularly, that he will achieve those purposes. The promise given to Abraham has not changed nor has it been taken back.

This section is rounded off with Deuteronomy. The Israelites are back again on the borders of the Promised Land. Moses, who by this time knows that he will not be joining them there, is determined that they will not make a mess of things this time, and so he makes a long and impassioned speech which reminds them of all that God has done and all that he expects of them. Always, in the background, is the special relationship: God has chosen and delivered his people and is about to establish them in a new land. But if they are to bring blessing to the nations, they will have to live in obedience to God rather than pleasing themselves. During their time in the desert they have often tried to live without God, complained, even wanted to go back to Egypt. This spirit of ingratitude and independence has marked the human race since Eden and still does. But God does not give up on them.

Laws are not just about rules that we have to keep; they are part of what it means to be God's special people. Relationships have always mattered more to God than rules. But if God's people persist in breaking the rules, it will break the relationship.

These books of the Law, then, are about far more than rules. Here we find the patterns which run through the rest of the Bible. Creation and sin, promise and rebellion, hope and deliverance – all are here. God's promise to bless the world through the descendants of Abraham, his establishment of his people and the system of worship and sacrifice will all, in time, find their fulfilment in Jesus – but that lies in the future. First, there are other lands for us to explore.

Bible books – history

Joshua	Israel enter the land and take possession of (most of) it.
Judges	Repeated cycles of disobedience, calls to return in the form of foreign oppression and deliverance through individuals called judges.
Ruth	Not really history in the proper sense, but the story of how Naomi returns to Israel after going to Moab in a famine. It can be seen as a love story, or as showing that foreigners have a place in God's plan for his people. Ruth is also named in the line of Jesus' ancestors (see Matthew 1:5).
1 and 2 Samuel	The end of the period of the judges, the appointment of the first king, Saul, and the stories of David, who is to be the second king.
1 and 2 Kings	Israel splits into two, the stories of a succession of kings and battles culminating in the destruction of the northern kingdom of Israel in 722 BC and the exile of the southern kingdom of Judah in 587 BC.
1 and 2 Chronicles	Repeats much of the material from Kings, but only for Judah with a special emphasis on the role of the king, worship and the priests.
Ezra	The initial return to the land in 538 BC, the rebuilding of the Temple and Ezra's return in 458 BC.
Nehemiah	Reforms under Ezra and Nehemiah who comes to Jerusalem in 445 BC.
Esther	Life under later Persian rule with the story of God preserving his people through Esther.

Boring old history?

People have conflicting views about history. To Henry Ford it was 'all bunk'. The past is a foreign country; we don't know how to make sense of what goes on. There are strange names and strange customs; it is hard to see how any of it might affect us today. But we are all, as individuals and as nations, what we are because of our history. We cannot ignore our past for it helps us to understand who we are today. Why else do so many people spend time and money exploring their family trees?

History is the arena in which God is at work. Look carefully and you will see his hand everywhere. While we cannot instantly assume that he will work in exactly the same way today as he did at some point in the past, we can learn a lot about who he is and what he does by looking at history. In the original Hebrew Old Testament, the Bible or *Tanakh*, still used by Jews, the books that we call historical (see opposite) are called the Former Prophets (the books that we call prophets are known as the Latter Prophets). That is because while they are history, they are history written with a purpose – to show what God is doing in the world and to explain what that means. These are not the only books in which we find history – Genesis, Exodus and Numbers contain a good deal, as do some of the prophets.

The people we meet in these books live in a very different world to ours, but they have similar hopes and fears, they struggle as we do with broken relationships, with failure to be true to others and to God, and they have great experiences of

God's grace. These books speak to us at two levels. They tell the ongoing story of God at work among his people and they show us how people like ourselves get caught up in those plans and move them forward through obedience or disobedience. One thing we learn is that although God's people often get it wrong, God's plans are never thwarted.

The story picks up where Deuteronomy leaves off. Moses hands over to Joshua whom we have met before as one of the 12 spies who went into the Promised Land. Of the 12, only he and Caleb were prepared to trust God, making him an ideal person to lead the people into the land. He had been Moses' assistant for some time, learning 'on the job'. The book which bears his name, Joshua, tells the story. More spies go in and are hidden by a prostitute who is later spared when Jericho is taken. This provides us with an unexpected link with the story of Jesus, for this same Rahab, a woman of dubious morality and not one of Abraham's descendants, is included in the list of Jesus' ancestors. God does not always work in the way that we would expect and does not always choose to work through the people of whom we would approve. The conquest of the land is not entirely straightforward. Some cities are conquered easily, others provide more resistance. Stories like the capture of Jericho are well known – deservedly so, for it is story which illustrates one of the central themes, making it clear that the victory is not the work of military armies, but of God. The idea that God uses the weak, the insignificant and the foolish is one we shall meet again when we get to the New Testament. By the end of Joshua, Israel is in occupation and the land has been divided up between the various tribes. But there is still work to be done. Many of the other nations have retained a foothold and this will cause problems in the years ahead.

Why all the killing?

Many of the historical books, Joshua in particular, present a problem for modern readers: there is just too much slaughter, much of it including women and children. What are we to make of this? This is a question to which there is no final answer, but we can find a few pointers. In the first place we must recognise that it reflects the times; they were brutal and lacked some of our sensitivities (although we could hardly claim that the last 100 years has shown any greater signs of civilisation or human kindness). The nations in the land were extremely evil and oppressive, with a range of worship practices including human sacrifice and ritual prostitution. If **Israel** were to have any chance of being the distinctive people that God wanted them to be – not for their benefit, but for the benefit of the whole world – it was necessary that all forms of temptation be removed. All of us want to live in a moral universe in which good triumphs over evil. The trouble is that we are not always willing to pay the price – we want evil eradicated but in a painless way, and it may not be that easy. It is clear that God held off as long as he could, but there always comes a time when, in order to establish justice and remove oppression, he must act. None of this gives a complete answer, but we can take refuge in the knowledge that in Jesus, God has chosen a different way to deal with the evil in the world.

Judges takes us into a world of failure. Time and time again **Israel** deserts God. Time and time again, he allows them to fall into their enemies' hands as a way of calling them back. Time and time again they turn back and cry out to God. Time and time again God brings along a leader who will deliver them. In many parts of our world the term 'judge' suggests a picture of aged individuals in wigs sitting in courtrooms, but these judges were dynamic leaders who could determine God's will, convey it to the people and lead them forward, delivering them from the oppressor. This cycle of failure, repentance and restoration acts as a reminder that left to our own devices we humans get it wrong and that it is only when God acts that we find hope and freedom. This is a theme which we saw in the exodus and will see again. It is a theme which finds its fullest expression in Jesus.

The books of Samuel take us through the last of the judges, Samuel, and on to the appointment of a king. In some ways this is seen as a bad move. God should really be the only king in Israel, and from one angle the call for a king is a rejection of God and a desire to be like everyone else, forgetting again that the nation of Israel is meant to be different. But viewed from another angle, the king becomes God's leader for the nation. There are good kings and bad kings, but the ideal is that they represent God's rule.

The first king, Saul, gets off to a good start but soon decides he could do things better his own way than going God's way – by now, a familiar story. The second, David, achieves a great deal. He first demonstrates his dependence on God by relying on him in the battle with Goliath. But he is far from perfect: a man who can write beautiful praise songs (many of which are found in the book of Psalms), and worship God without inhibitions, yet also a man who can commit adultery and murder. Perhaps, most surprisingly, David is seen as the ideal king. God renews his **covenant** with him, promising to establish his dynasty for ever as the rulers of **Israel**. Here again the bigger picture can be seen. In the middle of all this mess and failure, God is preparing for a future king – a descendant of David who would rule as God intended; that king, of course, is the **Messiah**, Jesus. This hope is seen more strongly as we move forward – but David, for all his failures, is the ideal who shapes the vision of the future. At least he is big enough to recognise his failure and to look for God's forgiveness.

David's failure has other consequences. His family is a mess. One son, Absalom, rebels and takes over the throne – and David has a brief spell on the run. Another, Amnon, rapes his half-sister. Even Solomon, who succeeds his father and is renowned for his wisdom, is hardly a model of good behaviour. In trying to show his power and status, he behaves like every other ancient monarch, accumulating 700 wives and 300 concubines – a pretty impressive harem by any standards! But in this lay his downfall. Many of the marriages are politically motivated, designed to bring influence with neighbouring powers, and the foreign wives bring foreign gods. Once again the scene is set for Israel to move away from God.

Judah and Israel – the divided kingdom

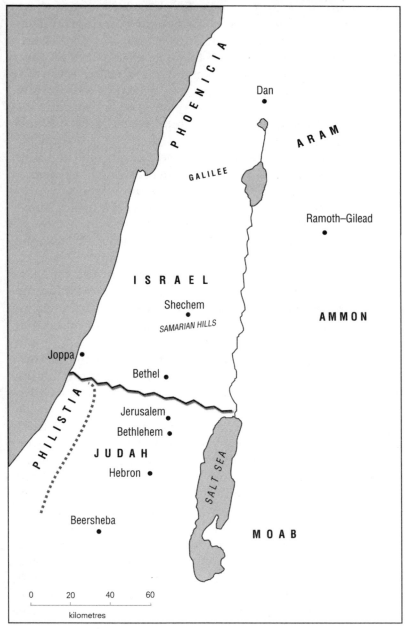

Solomon's son is determined to follow in his father's footsteps and, drunk with power, alienates half the country and a split results. Ten of the original twelve tribes go their own way and set up a new kingdom. With its capital in Samaria, the northern kingdom is now called Israel, and the southern one is called Judah. The first king in the north, Jeroboam, set up two calves in a new worship centre. He is for ever after referred to as 'Jeroboam son of Nebat, who caused Israel to sin' (eg 1 Kings 22:52) – not the best way to be remembered.

In the north, it is pretty much downhill from here on. It is a sad story of worshipping other gods, social breakdown, oppression and injustice. Prophets like Elijah, Elisha and Amos do all they can to bring the people to their senses. There are brief glimpses of what might have been. Finally, Samaria falls and they are overrun by the Assyrians who import other nationalities so that there is no chance of Israel being re-established. This is the origin of the Samaritan problem that we meet over 700 years later in the Gospels (eg John 4:19). The Jews' resentment against Samaritans, which goes back to the rebellion, is made worse by the idolatry, and is sealed when foreigners are introduced, resulting in the loss of national identity.

The story in the south, Judah, is better – but not much. There are kings who introduce foreign gods. There are others, notably Hezekiah and Josiah, who introduce reforms, but it is only ever skin-deep. There seems to be a destructive streak in the people who are determined to do things their way rather than God's way. Into this scenario various prophets speak of God's love, but also of God's hatred of injustice and idolatry, and his grief when his people worship other things. That story must wait for another day. In the end, the repeated failure to hear and return leads to Judah being conquered by Babylon and taken into exile.

It may look as though all is lost with **Israel** obliterated, Judah crushed and the significant members of society in exile. This was how they felt and the question with which they struggled. We shall see how they dealt with it when we come to look at the psalms and some of the prophets. In Babylon, however, Daniel and his friends demonstrate that it is possible to do things in a different way and be faithful to God even in difficult circumstances. Ezekiel looks forward to a time when God will put things right. Despite the failure of God's people and apparent disaster, God has not lost sight of his promise to Abraham.

The exile ends when there is a change in the power structures. Babylon is defeated by Persia, and the Persian king, Cyrus, lets the people return home. It was never going to be easy. They struggle to rebuild with limited resources and limited motivation. Within about twenty-three years the Temple has been rebuilt, but it was never their top priority and it takes some strong words from Haggai and Zechariah to keep them working on it. Almost 100 years pass before Ezra arrives, followed a few years later by Nehemiah, to find the city of Jerusalem still in a mess and the people with little hope. Under their leadership things improve for a time and there is a new sense of what God can do.

This is where we leave the history. There is now a period of almost 400 years of which the Bible tells us little. The returning settlers remain, for the most part, a small and struggling group under the control of Persia then of Greece before being caught between the two divided parts of the Greek empire. There is a brief period in the second century during which they achieve independence. While much worship is still centred on the rebuilt Temple in Jerusalem, the Jews are now dispersed throughout the world, and the synagogue becomes more significant. Groups like the Pharisees and the Sadducees, whom we meet in the New Testament, develop. Worship for many shifts from being centred on **sacrifice** to being centred on the Law, and the prophets and the psalms gradually become the 'hymn book'. God's revelation of himself, recorded in the pages of what we know as the Old Testament, was at the heart of their ongoing faith and life. That is the background to the New Testament to which we will later turn; but before that, we must look at other elements of these books (or, more accurately, scrolls) which meant so much to them.

Bible books – prophets

WHO?	WHEN?	WHERE?
Isaiah	740–700 BC	South – Judah
Jeremiah	626–587 BC	South – Judah
Ezekiel	593–570 BC	Exile in Babylon
Daniel	604–535 BC	Exile in Babylon
Hosea	755–722 BC	North – Israel
Joel	Uncertain	
Amos	760 BC	North – Israel
Obadiah	Possibly c 587 BC	South – Judah
Jonah	760 BC	Nineveh
Micah	740–690 BC	South – Judah
Nahum	660–612 BC	South – Judah
Habakkuk	605 BC	South – Judah
Zephaniah	630–620 BC	South – Judah
Haggai	520 BC	South – Judah
Zechariah	529–500 BC	South – Judah
Malachi	450 BC	South – Judah

God's spokesmen

Prophets are often misunderstood. That was literally true for those who brought a message from God, only to find themselves ridiculed, abused, rejected, imprisoned and killed. It is true in a different sense today. But we too can misunderstand the prophets. In everyday language, the name suggests those who foretell the future. The Old Testament prophets do look into the future, but their primary role is to interpret the present and to bring God's perspective on society.

We first meet the term when Abraham is described as a prophet in Genesis 20:7. This seems to suggest that he is a man close to God who can speak for God. In Exodus 7:1 Aaron is described as Moses' prophet. Moses has been protesting that he is not a good speaker so God gives him someone who will speak for him. This describes the primary role of the prophet – to speak for another. The prophets are often described as messengers of God and they themselves speak of the word of God coming to them.

Prophets crop up in the historical books – the best known are Elijah and Elisha, but there are others. Elijah's role was to bring God's word to Ahab. Elisha was his successor and had a similar role. Elisha seems to have had others around him, perhaps as trainees. Other prophets appear, often, like Elijah, to confront kings. One of the most notable examples is Nathan coming to David and pointing out his sin of adultery and murder (2 Samuel 12:1–14). The role is not confined to men; Miriam (Exodus 15:20), Deborah (Judges 4:4) and Huldah (2 Kings 22:14) are all described as prophetesses.

However, as we take in the whole picture of the Bible we see a large block of books by those who are sometimes called the 'writing prophets'. These books take up the last section of the Old Testament in our English Bibles. The prophets who wrote them fulfil the same role as those we have met in the historical books. Indeed, Isaiah gets several mentions in Kings and Chronicles (2 Kings 19,20; 2 Chronicles 26:22, 32:32), Jeremiah is mentioned in 2 Chronicles 35:25; 36:12,21,22, and Jonah in 2 Kings 14:25. They are often divided into the major prophets (Isaiah, Jeremiah and Ezekiel), and the minor prophets (the books of Daniel through to Malachi). This is a description of length rather than importance. In the Hebrew scriptures, Hosea to Malachi form one book, the Book of the Twelve, perhaps because they fitted on one scroll; Daniel is included in 'the writings' (see 'The contents of the Bible', p37,38).

The prophets were active over a period of time from about 760 BC to about 460 BC. They speak out in different situations: some to the southern kingdom of Judah, some to the northern kingdom of Israel, others in exile, Jonah in Nineveh. In some cases we can be reasonably certain about dates, but in others we don't know. The table on page 60 shows who was operating where and when.

The earliest prophetic writings come from the middle of the eighth century. In both north and south, the situation is much the same: there is economic prosperity but social breakdown and spiritual confusion. In the north, the situation is made worse by the calf idols made by King Jeroboam at the time of the breakaway (1 Kings 12:25–33), which simply add to the spiritual confusion. In their different ways, Isaiah, Micah, Amos and Hosea address this situation. They see a clear link between the failure to worship God and the oppression and injustice in their society. The nation will be judged both for its departure from God and for its rampant injustice. But even amidst this gloom there is a sense of hope. Hosea speaks powerfully of the love which God has for his people which will never change. In calling the people to turn back to God, he emphasises that God is always ready to receive them. Each of the others, in different ways, speak of restoration beyond judgement.

The book of Isaiah presents special problems. There is a distinctly different note from chapter 40 onwards. While the earlier chapters relate to the situation in Jerusalem and look forward to a time of destruction unless behaviour changes, the later chapters speak of a time when the people are in exile and look forward to a return. This has led many scholars to assume that they were written by a later, anonymous prophet, but there are many similarities in thought, message and language, and there is no reason why God should not have given these messages of hope to Isaiah even though they speak most effectively to a future generation.

Jeremiah is active in the years immediately before the fall of Jerusalem. He exposes the shallowness of the people's faith and predicts disaster. Like the earlier prophets, he too sees hope beyond it. He speaks of a new **covenant** which God will make with his people – not a set of external laws, but a new inner motivation to obey and know God (Jeremiah 31:33). Ezekiel, speaking during the exile, sees the corruption that has led to the glory of God leaving Jerusalem (Ezekiel 10,11), but looks forward to a restored Jerusalem and a restored Temple (Ezekiel 39:21 – 48:35). Haggai and Zechariah were active after the return from exile and their main concern is that the people are not giving enough attention to God and the rebuilding of the Temple. It would seem that the lessons of the exile have not been learned. When we come to Malachi, the problems still remain, with the people not giving God right worship. Like the others, he can look forward to something new that God will do when a messenger comes to the Temple. Here, as so often, the goal of the prophets' new hope is focused on Jesus.

This highlights the central theme of the prophets. On the one hand, they call the people back to their **covenant** responsibilities. They remind them of their need to love God and neighbour if they are to enjoy the land that God has given them. They point out that God's people cannot take him for granted. Jeremiah, in a particularly powerful passage, tells them that trusting in the presence of the Temple and the promise of God will do nothing for them if they fail to obey him.

> Do not trust in deceptive words and say, 'This is the temple of the LORD, the temple of the LORD, the temple of the LORD!' If you really change your ways and your actions and deal with each other justly, if you do not oppress the alien, the fatherless or the widow and do not shed innocent blood in this place, and if you do not follow other gods to your own harm, then I will let you live in this place, in the land I gave to your forefathers for ever and ever. But look, you are trusting in deceptive words that are worthless.
>
> *Jeremiah 7:4-8*

In an equally powerful passage, Amos points out that their worship is utterly distasteful to God because their lives are not right.

> I hate, I despise your religious feasts;
>> I cannot stand your assemblies.
> Even though you bring me burnt offerings and grain offerings,
>> I will not accept them.
> Though you bring choice fellowship offerings,
>> I will have no regard for them.
> Away with the noise of your songs!
>> I will not listen to the music of your harps.
> But let justice roll on like a river,
>> righteousness like a never-failing stream!
>
> *Amos 5:21–24*

Throughout, there is also a call to come back to God. Many of the prophets' sermons take the form, 'Unless you change, judgement will come...' However, even as they call the people back there seems to be a growing sense that the people will not respond. God has to do something new if there is to be any hope. The hopes that had been invested in the land and then in the kings as a fulfilment of the promise to Abraham are fading; something more and something deeper is needed. **Israel** had been called as a witness to show the nations something of the power, justice and love of God, but had failed. If God's promise to bless the nations through Abraham is to be fulfilled, a new way will have to be found. That, at least, would have been their perspective. From God's perspective, however, everything is on track.

One of the notes that shine through the prophetic writings is of the future coming of one who will be all that Israel has not been. Isaiah speaks of the Servant of the Lord (eg Isaiah 49:3). This figure sometimes seems to be Israel, and sometimes an individual but, in the final analysis, no one quite matches up. We are left looking into the future for one who will proclaim justice to the nations, for one who will deal with the sin and failure of the people. Jesus specifically takes the words of Isaiah 42:1–4 which speak of the servant who will 'bring justice to the nations' and applies them to himself in Matthew 12:15–21.

The prophets look forward to a time when God will come to rule his people in a new way: Isaiah's vision of the wolf and the lamb living together (Isaiah 11:6); Micah's and Isaiah's visions of universal peace, of swords being made into ploughs and of everyone sitting under their own vines and fig-trees (Isaiah 2:1–4; Micah 4:1–5); Zechariah's vision of city streets filled with children playing (Zechariah 8:5) – all these are visions of a future kingdom, dimly seen, but not yet realised. In Isaiah's servant and in Malachi's one who will come to the Temple (Malachi 3:1), in Ezekiel's promise of one nation ruled over by David (Ezekiel 37:22–24) and in Zechariah's coming king, 'righteous and having salvation, gentle and riding on a donkey, on a colt, the foal of a donkey' (Zechariah 9:9), we glimpse, in an increasingly clear way, the nature of the one who will come.

In Isaiah 53 we are shown how human sin will be finally dealt with:

> Surely he took up our infirmities
>   and carried our sorrows,
> yet we considered him stricken by God,
>   smitten by him, and afflicted.
> But he was pierced for our transgressions,

he was crushed for our iniquities;
the punishment that brought us peace was upon him,
and by his wounds we are healed.
We all, like sheep, have gone astray,
each of us has turned to his own way;
and the Lord has laid on him
the iniquity of us all.

Isaiah 53:4–6

It is becoming clear that only Jesus can meet all these requirements. Just as he takes the words of Isaiah 42 and applies them to himself, so he takes the words of Isaiah 61 and applies them to himself too:

The Spirit of the Lord is on me,
because he has anointed me
to preach good news to the poor.
He has sent me to proclaim freedom for the prisoners
and recovery of sight for the blind,
to release the oppressed,
to proclaim the year of the Lord's favour.

Luke 4:18–19

We are left in no doubt. The hopes that the prophets begin to perceive beyond the oppression, injustice, failure and idolatry of their present reality are summed up in the one whom God will send. In him, the supreme descendant of Abraham, all the nations of the world will be blessed and all the promises of God fulfilled.

All human life is there

An aerial view of the earth sometimes reveals what looks rather a rather shapeless block of land. Peaks and valleys, deserts and forests, lakes and scrubland all jumbled together. There is something similar in our biblical landscape. This is the world of wisdom: Proverbs, Job, Ecclesiastes and the Song of Songs.

These books wrestle with life the way it is. They are for anyone who has ever tried to make sense of life and not quite come up with all the answers. Sometimes life does make sense, everything fits together and all is well; the answers are simple and straightforward. That is the world of Proverbs. But there are other times when our worlds fall apart and none of the answers make sense. That is the world of Job. There are also times when intellectual doubts creep in and we fear that we are losing our moorings. That is the world of Ecclesiastes. To complete the picture, there is the Song of Songs for those times when love takes over and nothing else matters.

Psalms are not really part of this section. In many ways they are section all of their own, but as they cover some similar ground it is worth looking at them here. The psalms reflect all of these moods and struggles in different ways.

What are we to make of all of this? Where might it fit into our bigger plan? These books demonstrate for us that all of human life is lived out in God's presence. Nothing lies outside God's concern. It is the world, with all the hopes, fears and failures that mark our lives, that God is sorting out. God is interested in all that goes to make up our everyday world and he is going to redeem and restore all of it.

Proverbs consists mainly of short, pithy observations about the way that life is. They concern friendship and money, food and work, wise leadership and foolish behaviour. Many have found their way into everyday language. They do not give us a complete description of the way things are. Sometimes we will read them with a wry grin, identifying with the sentiments; at other times we will be inwardly crying out, 'It isn't that simple!' There are wise and sensible ways to live. The early chapters highlight the difference between wisdom and folly. The wise way is God's way. At times in these early chapters, especially in chapter 8, wisdom is described in language that makes it sound human. Wisdom is described as sharing with God in the work of creation, underlining the fact that the creation speaks of God's wisdom.

> I was there when he set the heavens in place,
>> when he marked out the horizon on the face of the deep,
> when he established the clouds above
>> and fixed securely the fountains of the deep,
> when he gave the sea its boundary
>> so that the waters would not overstep his command,
> and when he marked out the foundations of the earth.
>> Then I was the craftsman at his side.
> I was filled with delight day after day,
>> rejoicing always in his presence,
> rejoicing in his whole world
>> and delighting in mankind.
>
> *Proverbs 8:27–31*

When we see this in the light of the opening words of John's Gospel, 'Through him all things were made; without him nothing was made that has been made' (John 1:3), we can see a deeper significance. John is speaking of the Word of God, who has come among us as Jesus. Paul speaks of Jesus as the wisdom of God (1 Corinthians 1:24), so even in this we can see hints of what God is doing. All true wisdom comes to us from Christ, even if we are unaware of it.

Job, by contrast, struggles with life that doesn't fit the expectations. He loses everything and has friends who assure him repeatedly that this is his fault. This was the standard answer: behave well and all will go right; behave badly and all will go wrong. Everything has gone wrong for Job and so he must have sinned. Job, however, protests his innocence. His speeches are a cry to God for vindication – he wants to come before God and plead his cause. When God finally appears, it is to confront Job with God's power, majesty and glory. In the face of this, Job has no answer. The story shows us that while there may be no final answer to the problems caused by evil, and questions about why good people suffer, it all still happens under God's control. In longing for vindication, Job is reaching for something that will only be found when Jesus comes. God's answer to these questions is to be found in him.

Ecclesiastes shares some of Job's questioning, but in a more philosophical way. The writer has tried everything, but nothing brings satisfaction – something that the Rolling Stones were to discover some years later ('I ain't got no satisfaction')! Money, learning, relationships – none can give what he wants. His final conclusion is that only in seeking out God can true satisfaction be found. For him this seems a tentative conclusion, but it highlights the message of wisdom. Life lived without reference to God is pointless. True wisdom can only be found in God and reaches its fullest expression in Jesus.

The Song of Songs is something else. Few books have generated so much discussion. Some have questioned whether it should be in the Bible at all. Others have regarded it as one of the most important books there is. At face value, it is a collection of explicit love poems (far more explicit than appears in most English translations). Who the various characters are – indeed how many there are – is uncertain, but one thing is clear: this is a beautiful celebration of erotic love. Sex is a great gift of God when used wisely and in the right context, a truth the Church has not always grasped. The fact that this book is in the Bible at all reminds us again that the whole of life, including our sexuality, is lived out under God's gaze. It is this world that he is working in; it is this human race that he is saving; and it is this physical creation that he is restoring. There is no place in Christian thinking for the idea that the physical side of life, in any sense, is evil – all is created by God, all will be redeemed and restored by God.

Into this world of struggle and hope, joy and fear, faith and doubt the book of Psalms speaks with a clear voice. Composed over a long period and by many different authors, it contains songs that cover the whole of life. These, in time, became the hymns of the Jewish people and, later, a central part of the worship of the Christian Church. But what a hymn book! Even a quick glance will reveal that there are songs here that are unlike any that we sing in our churches today.

There are songs that express the pain of rejection:

> Scorn has broken my heart
> > and has left me helpless;
> I looked for sympathy, but there was none,
> > for comforters, but I found none.
>
> *Psalm 69:20*

There are songs that express profound confidence in God:

> The LORD is my rock, my fortress and my deliverer;
> my God is my rock, in whom I take refuge.
> He is my shield and the horn of my salvation, my stronghold.
>
> *Psalm 18:2*

Some of them start with the pain and move to a position of faith as the writer comes to an understanding of God:

> But as for me, my feet had almost slipped;
> > I had nearly lost my foothold.
> For I envied the arrogant
> > when I saw the prosperity of the wicked.
>
> ...

My flesh and my heart may fail,
>   but God is the strength of my heart
>   and my portion for ever.

Psalm 73:2,3,26

We might be more familiar with the songs of thanksgiving and praise, with the songs that recall all that God has done for his people, or celebrate the beauty of creation, but we will gasp at the anger behind such sentiments as:

O Daughter of Babylon, doomed to destruction,
>   happy is he who repays you
>   for what you have done to us –
he who seizes your infants
>   and dashes them against the rocks.

Psalm 137:8,9

As sensitive people, we find this horrifying. Here, the Bible seems to approve of such sentiments. We need to stand back. We know that in the bigger plan God does not approve of such violence and vindictive statements. But here, it gives us the encouragement to be honest with God about the way that we feel, to express to him both praise and anger, love and despair. The psalms give us language in which we can give vent to a full range of human emotions.

Running through the Psalms, with all their variety, is the thought that God has delivered his people and is with them. The writers may struggle with God's apparent absence and with the pain of life but they never finally lose sight of the fact that only God can give any real hope. Like the prophets, some of the psalms begin to look beyond the present situation. There are psalms which celebrate God's reign and convey the sense that there is more to come in the future (eg Psalm 93). Some of the psalms of pain and rejection look to a time when God himself will enter into human rejection and pain and deal with it once and for all (eg Psalm 22).

These books show us a people living with both a sense of

God's presence in the daily reality of life while longing for something more. Those who put them together knew that God was committed to them and to his purposes for the world. They knew that there were promises yet to be fulfilled. That is not the full story of the Old Testament, but it is one of the keys. God has set something in motion that cannot be stopped; not all is seen yet, but all is coming. There is a sense of waiting, of longing. There is, even among the failure and the judgement, a sense that God will make all things good. To that part of the story we now turn.

The King is here

We have explored God's act of creation, we have seen humanity reject God and we have seen the centuries of preparation for God's work of restoration. We have left the Old Testament with a sense of promise, of unfulfilled longing. We have seen God choose Israel not just for its own sake but to bring blessing to the world. We have seen its failure, and we have seen new hope emerging. In fact, God's plans were deeper and more wonderful than any of those who had listened, obeyed and struggled in the Old Testament era could have imagined. Later in the New Testament, Paul writes about 'the mystery that has been kept hidden for ages and generations, but is now disclosed to the saints' (Colossians 1:26). He doesn't mean something mysterious or puzzling in the sense that we might use the word. The mystery is something that has been hidden away waiting for the right moment – like the Christmas presents hidden in all manner of places around our house until Christmas morning, when all is revealed.

Indeed, very like Christmas morning – for that is where our next exploration begins. Of the four Gospels, only Matthew and Luke have any details about Jesus before his ministry begins. Matthew starts in what seems to us an unlikely way, with a long list of names. Why? Because for him, it is important to set Jesus in the long-term plan of God. He starts with Abraham, reminding us of the promise that we have met before, to bless all nations through his descendants; it is here that this is finally and completely fulfilled. Along the way, as we trace the line, we meet some unlikely people, those who have failed and those who do not come from Israel. Luke does something similar, but a little later in his account, and he goes back to Adam, underlining the fact that Jesus has come for all humanity.

The story of Jesus' birth is well known, although it seems that we find it hard to separate the historical fact from the nice stories that have accumulated over the years. At its simplest, it is the story of a young girl called to give birth to the one whom God had promised, of an initially surprised and suspicious fiancé, of a humble birth in an unlikely town (but one with a good kingly pedigree, for this was David's hometown). Around this core are rejoicing angels announcing that the moment has come, wise men travelling from the East, hinting again that this was good news for the nations and not just for Israel, and a jealous king. Matthew reminds us time and time again that this has happened to fulfil the promise of the Old Testament. Luke describes this birth as good news.

Good news

The idea of good news has a long history with a rich Old Testament background. Isaiah 52:7 looks forward to the coming of one who will bring good news, in the immediate context of the return from exile. Later, Isaiah speaks of one who will come to preach good news to the poor (Isaiah 61:1). The related verb is used in verses like Psalm 96:2 to announce the good news of God's salvation. It was associated with the announcement of victory (2 Samuel 18:20). It was associated with a new king being crowned. In the Roman world, it was used to refer to the messages that came from the oracles, those who were believed to speak for the gods. It was also used to herald the birth of a son in the imperial household at a time when the emperors were seeing themselves as gods.

So the background suggests, to both Jew and Gentile, new divine activity. In the Gospels, the birth of Jesus is proclaimed as good news (Luke 2:10), and Jesus describes his message about the **kingdom** as good news (Luke 4:43; Mark 1:14,15). In his reply to John the Baptist, he picks up the words of Isaiah 61:1,2, applying them to himself. Jesus sends his disciples out to tell others the good news (Mark 16:15).

Paul uses the term over 80 times. In many versions it is translated 'gospel', the Old English word for good news, which became a widely-used term within the Christian Church. For him, it is the message he preaches which has the power to save those who believe (Romans 1:16).

Luke is the only writer to give us a glimpse into the early years of Jesus. His visit to the Temple at the age of 12 – probably the year before he would have officially entered into manhood – shows that, even at this age, Jesus is beginning to have a clear sense of his identity. He is not on earth simply to please himself. He must be doing what his Father wants (Luke 2:49), a note that will repeat at the end of his life (Luke 22:42). Mark starts his Gospel with the stark announcement, 'The beginning of the gospel about Jesus Christ, the Son of God' (Mark 1:1) before going on to quote from Malachi and Isaiah:

I will send my messenger ahead of you,
    who will prepare your way –
a voice of one calling in the desert,
'Prepare the way for the Lord,
    make straight paths for him.'
Mark 1:2,3

Where does all this leave us? With the clear understanding that the Gospel writers had no doubt that, with the coming of Jesus, all that God had promised had come to pass. He had come to put everything right.

Matthew, Mark and Luke all record Jesus' baptism and temptation. The baptism shows that he is fully human, one with us, and also reveals his divine identity. He then goes straight into the desert to face the full force of temptation and reveals his power over it. This shows that he is, as the writer of Hebrews puts it, 'one who has been tempted in every way, just as we are' (Hebrews 4:15). Only one who has been through what we experience and who understands, only one who is fully man and fully God could put things back together. The promise has been of God coming to his people in a new way, of a new king who would rule justly and rightly, of a servant who would bring **good news**.

We have already seen how Jesus, right at the start of his public ministry, stands in the synagogue at Nazareth, reads from the scroll of Isaiah 61, and announces that he has come in fulfilment of the promise (see Luke 4:16–21). He will later use other verses from the Old Testament prophets to describe his work. From the start, he defines himself and his ministry in terms that his contemporaries would have recognised from the Old Testament.

In picking up Isaiah's words, Jesus describes himself as the anointed one or **Messiah**. He announces that his coming is the **good news** that the people have long awaited, and he brings freedom. In the announcement of freedom there are echoes of the exodus. God brought his people out of Egypt where they had been slaves. So, the exodus, whereby God saved his people, becomes a model for what he is now about to do in Jesus. In the book of Exodus, there is a strong note of redemption – the people have been freed at a cost. We shall discover that the same is true in the freedom that God is bringing through Jesus.

The arrival of Jesus brings in 'the year of the Lord's favour'. This is the Year of Jubilee in which debts were written off and slaves freed (Leviticus 25:8–54). It was designed to ensure that no one ended up in permanent slavery and that land never passed permanently out of the original family line. Behind it all was the sense that all belonged to God and was entrusted to his people to look after. The Year of Jubilee was a time of restoration. Jesus brings the ultimate restoration.

With all this rich Old Testament imagery, Jesus announces his **mission**. He has come to bring healing, freedom and restoration. God's age-old plan is finally coming to fruition. Our early view of one single whole was correct – all of this fits together to form one big picture. Jesus' life and teaching bears this out. His primary message is that the **kingdom** has come – in other words, God is now ruling his people.

Kingdom

We think of a kingdom as a country – an area ruled by a king. But in the Bible, the kingdom of God is not about a physical area but about the active rule of God, about God making his presence known as King. The background lies in the Old Testament kings who ruled for God but failed to do as he required. This leads to the expectation that one day God will come and will rule his people in a new way. In the thinking of Judaism this came to be seen as 'the Age to Come'. Jesus tells us that in him that time has come, that God is now ruling his people (Mark 1:15; Luke 11:20). Matthew nearly always uses the phrase 'the kingdom of heaven' because he was writing for a Jewish audience and for them the name of God was too sacred to be used, so they often substituted 'heaven'. When Jesus sends the disciples out, it is to spread the good news of the kingdom (Luke 9:1-6; 10:1–12). And yet at the same time, the kingdom is still to come (Luke 22:16,18). In Jesus, God has come to his people in a new way: through his life, death and resurrection the kingdom has come, but not yet in all its fullness. There will come a day when all will see and recognise the King, but that is not yet. There is an overlap and we live in that time. This explains why all is not yet as it will be, nor as God intends it to be.

Much of Jesus' teaching, especially in the parables, is about the nature of the kingdom, about the way in which the Age to Come exists alongside the present age. In Jesus, God's future has invaded the present. For those who can see it, the parables are a call to give allegiance to the King, and to live for him. The Sermon on the Mount (Matthew 5–7) is an explanation of what this means.

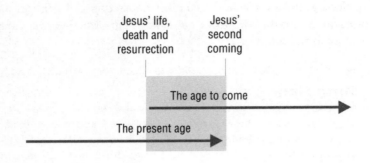

In Jesus, God's future has invaded the present

Jesus calls 12 men to share his life with him. In the ancient world, the rabbi, or teacher, would attract a group who chose to spend time with him, learning by observation, by listening, by trial and error, by dialogue. Their aim was to be as like the master as they could. The 12 are Jesus' disciples; the difference is that they have not chosen him as would normally have happened, but he has chosen them (John 15:16). The number '12' is significant. It reminds us of the 12 tribes of **Israel**. Jesus is establishing a renewed Israel. What the Old Testament servant had failed to do, Jesus, the promised servant of Isaiah, does, and he gathers around him a new community which will form the basis of the **kingdom** that he is establishing.

Jesus' miracles demonstrate that God is acting in a new way to bring in the kingdom. Of course, they demonstrate the love and the compassion of God, but they are more than that. They fulfil the Old Testament expectations of one who would bring healing, who would enable the lame to walk, the blind to see and the deaf to hear. Those who first witnessed this would have seen it all in a way that we perhaps do not. They also saw an authority they did not find elsewhere. When Jesus heals the paralysed man and forgives his sins (Mark 2:1–12), he is claiming an authority that belonged to God alone. His critics are quite right to see this, but they are unable to see the logical consequence of being right. When Jesus takes authority over demons, he is demonstrating the superior power of the kingdom. By taking authority over natural and supernatural forces, he is making a statement that he has authority which belongs only to God, and is putting down a marker: this broken, messed up, imperfect creation is going to be restored.

Jesus' claims inevitably lead to conflict. He threatens the status quo and challenges both the power of the Jewish leaders and the power of Rome. From a human point of view, he would be crucified as a rebel and a revolutionary. He simply could not be allowed to go on saying the things that he did or attracting the following that he did. The note of conflict is found in all the Gospels, but perhaps most clearly in John with the ever-present reference to conflict between light and darkness.

This conflict leads to Jesus' death, but that is not the whole story. A crucial change takes place after Peter recognises Jesus as **Messiah**, recounted in Matthew 16:13–16, Mark 8:27–29 and Luke 9:18–20. From this point on, Jesus teaches much more clearly about his impending death. It is not something imposed on him but something he embraces voluntarily and purposively (John 10:11,18). It is done for others (Mark 10:45); the idea of ransom implies that a price will be paid in order to bring freedom for others. His death will attract people to him (John 12:20–26,32); as Gentiles are involved his death, it will have an impact on more than just the Jewish nation. His death will, however, not be the final word; for he will be raised from death. The disciples don't grasp the full significance of all this. Their initial reaction is confusion. The thought of a dead **Messiah** does not ring true and, despite those they had seen raised by Jesus, the thought of his own resurrection does not sink in. By the time the events in the Gospels came to be recorded, all of Paul's letters had been written and much reflection on the significance of all this had taken place. The Gospel writers are less interested in developing the analysis than telling the story, but this should not lead to the conclusion that there is somehow a divide between the Gospels and the letters, or between Jesus and Paul. The very fact that the large part of all the Gospels is taken up with Jesus' last week and the account of the crucifixion and resurrection tell us that, for them, this was the key thing.

This is not to say that his life was in any way less significant. One cannot separate the one from the other. It was because God loved the world that he sent the Son (John 3:16). There is enormous significance in the fact that God came in flesh (John 1:14) – real human flesh and blood, sinew and bone, with genuine human feeling and emotion. This tells us the physical creation is good and that bodies are not somehow evil. It tells us that God knows and understands us. It tells us that not only has Jesus died for us, he has lived a life of perfect obedience for us, leaving us an example (1 Peter 2:21).

The Gospels can be trusted as accurate accounts. They accurately reflect the time in which they are set. There is no reason to doubt any of the accounts, unless one is predisposed to doubt the miraculous. There are other accounts such as the Gospel of Thomas, and from time to time people suggest that these are more reliable. In reality most of them are much later, much less convincing and don't even meet the claims that are made for them. The very fact that there are four Gospels in the New Testament and that they tell the same story with some variations and some different emphases is a confirmation of the truth.

The message is that God has come; that the world will never be the same again; that all people can now experience the freedom and healing that comes from knowing God, and that all this has been opened up to us by the death and resurrection of Jesus. There are still many questions we cannot ignore. If the kingdom has come and God is now ruling, why are there still so many problems and so much pain? Why, if the cross is the point where evil has been finally defeated, is there still so much of it about? The Gospels do not give us a final answer, but Jesus does promise that he will come back (John 14:1–4). The **kingdom** has come, but we do not yet see it in all its fullness. One day we will. But that is for another chapter.

Moving out

We live in a world of sequels and spin-offs. Every successful film demands a sequel – often not of the same quality as the original! Every TV series that pulls in the viewers demands another series or at least a repeat (or three). The Gospels are a bit like that, with the exception that the sequel is just as good.

Matthew ends his Gospel with Jesus leaving his disciples, having given them a task and promising to be with them:

> Therefore go and make disciples of all nations, baptising them in the name of the Father and of the Son and of the Holy Spirit, and teaching them to obey everything I have commanded you. And surely I am with you always, to the very end of the age.
> Matthew 28:19,20

Luke ends with him saying to them:

> You are witnesses of these things. I am going to send you what my Father has promised; but stay in the city until you have been clothed with power from on high.
> Luke 24:48,49

In John, Jesus sends his disciples out in the same way that he had been sent (John 20:21). The story has not ended; we are left expecting something more.

Acts tells us what happens next. It takes the story of God's work in the world and his plan to save humanity and shows what happens after Jesus returns to heaven. At the start of the book – which is really a sequel to Luke, being written by the same author and with the same audience in mind – Jesus returns to the Father (Acts 1:9) and the Holy Spirit comes to the small group of Jesus' followers (Acts 2:1–13). Jesus' command to his followers was to go and tell others what God had done. Luke sees this like ripples spreading out from Jerusalem:

> But you will receive power when the Holy Spirit comes on you; and you will be my witnesses in Jerusalem, and in all Judea and Samaria, and to the ends of the earth.
>
> *Acts 1:8.*

This is precisely what happens. The growth in Jerusalem is rapid. Persecution drives the believers out into the wider world and the message travels to Samaria as a result. Initially, the message goes mainly to Jews or people from other backgrounds who had started to worship God, but in Acts 10, Peter has the decisive vision which convinces him and the Church that God wants people of all nationalities to find him through Jesus. In the second half of Acts, we travel with Paul who goes throughout Asia Minor, the area we would now call Turkey, and later on, Greece, telling people about Jesus. Although his practice is to start in the Jewish synagogue, he soon realises that his calling is broader than that.

Acts is an exciting read – it has all the action of a thriller, all the local colour of a travel guide; it has pain and power, glory and suffering. The early Church grows rapidly, but faces continual opposition. God works in amazing ways. People are healed, raised from the dead, saved from shipwreck and snake bite; much of it reads very like the Gospels because God is continuing to establish a people who will show what he has done. In the Old Testament, **Israel** was God's witness to the world; the Church now fulfils that role. When Jesus called 12 disciples, he was sending out a message that just as he fulfilled the prophecies of the Old Testament about the King who would come, about the

The spread of the early church

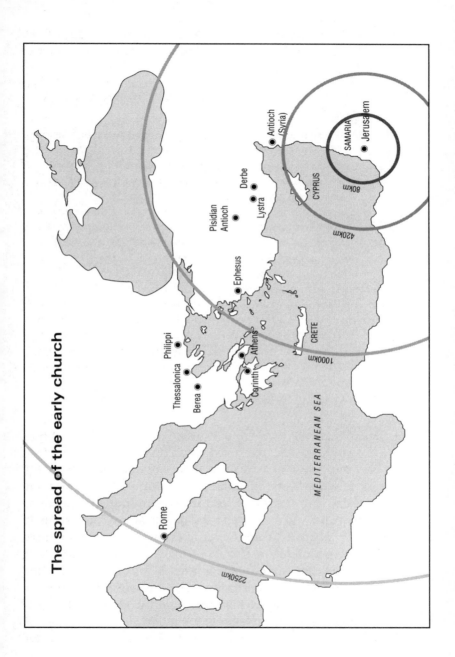

Servant of God, about the Prophet (Deuteronomy 18:15–18), so his people now continue to witness to God's saving activity, just as Israel had been called to do.

Mission

The word 'mission' is rare in the Bible – the NIV and the NRSV use it only once in the New Testament (Acts 12:25) and here it translates the word normally translated as 'service' – but the idea is everywhere. 'Mission' comes from the Latin word for sending. 'Apostle' derives from the Greek word for sending. Jesus sends his followers into the world just as the Father has sent him (John 20:21). Jesus was sent by the Father out of the Father's love for the world (John 3:16,17). That is the heart of mission – God reaching out to the world he made, now destroyed by sin. We sometimes think of mission as something we do, but it is always something God is doing, something in which he invites us to share. Paul, often described as the first missionary, felt that he had an obligation to tell others (Romans 1:14; 1 Corinthians 9:16), because God had called him and sent him (Acts 26:12–18). God's mission to the world – his desire to call all to himself – is a theme that runs from Genesis to Revelation.

Acts describes what happened. We can learn something of how God worked then, and that gives us pointers to the sort of God he is and the way that he will work in any age, but we cannot automatically use Acts as a model for the way things should happen today. But the same God is at work today and we can reasonably expect to see similar things happen at least some of the time. To discover what the early Church believed and how we, as followers of Jesus, should behave, we look to the letters rather than to Acts. What we see in Acts is mission in action, and we can be sure that the Church is called to mission. It is never our mission; it is always, as we have seen before, the outworking of God's mission, of his purposes for the world.

By the end of Acts – probably sometime in the early 60s of the first century – the message of Jesus has reached much of the Mediterranean world; a group of Christians has been established at the heart of the Roman Empire. It has been opposed by some Jews who cannot grasp the truth of what God has done, and it has been opposed by the power of Rome which sees it as a threat. (This in itself is an amazing thought. Rome, one of the most powerful empires the world had known at that point, fears that a small number of relatively powerless people could, by refusing to recognise the emperor as Lord, disrupt its life and undermine its power base.) Despite this opposition, the Church continues to grow.

The story does not end with the close of Acts; it continues through the ages and is still being written today. For us, the challenge of Acts is to join in with the mission of God. We will write our chapter of the story in our world and in our local situations.

This early Church also faces up to internal tensions. There are ethnic divisions, pressures on the leadership, questions about how to incorporate people from Gentile backgrounds. As they resolve these questions, they give us models for dealing with our own tensions as we encounter new situations in today's Church. In every age, despite external pressures and internal conflict, God ensures that his work moves forward.

Many new situations are encountered when Paul moves from the fairly well-known territory of the Jewish synagogue, where people know the Old Testament and worship one God, into the Gentile world. People here have no understanding of one God, no history of his law and no knowledge of how we are to be put right with him. Paul needs a different approach, an understanding of where others are coming from and of how a bridge can be built into their own thinking and experience. Responding to the call of God to take the message to all the peoples of the world, in fulfilment of the original promise to Abraham (as we saw earlier in Genesis 12:1–3) was not easy in practice:

> Though I am free and belong to no man, I make myself a slave to everyone, to win as many as possible. To the Jews I became like a Jew,

to win the Jews. To those under the law I became like one under the law (though I myself am not under the law), so as to win those under the law. To those not having the law I became like one not having the law (though I am not free from God's law but am under Christ's law), so as to win those not having the law. To the weak I became weak, to win the weak. I have become all things to all men so that by all possible means I might save some. I do all this for the sake of the gospel, that I may share in its blessings.

1 Corinthians 9:19–23

This still presents challenges for us as we speak to others who do not share our background understanding. But that is no reason for not working at it.

You've got mail

Letters have been replaced by more instant forms of communication: email and texting, podcasts and social networking websites. But there is still great pleasure in receiving a handwritten note from someone we love. It is more personal. When I was 15, I came home from Africa where my parents were missionaries. The only way we had of keeping in touch was letters – which took about a week to travel between me in London and the rest of the family in rural Malawi (and longer if no one was going the nine miles to the post office to pick up the mail). That may seem like a long time to those of us familiar with the instant communication of today; the letters of the New Testament took much longer to travel to their intended recipients.

Because we read them as part of a larger volume, it is easy to forget that everything from Romans to 3 John started life not as chapters in a book, but as letters written to individuals or churches in the first century. Like most letters, they have a purpose and they are based – or most of them are – on existing relationships.

The order of the books in the New Testament can be a little confusing. In fact, most of the letters were written before any of the Gospels or Acts. It is possible to slot the writing of at least some of the letters into the story of Acts, but others can be harder to fit.

So the earliest picture we get of church life is to be found in the letters. It is exciting and it is messy. These were early days after

Jesus. Many of those who have come to put their trust in him have very little understanding and their old beliefs and behavioural patterns live on. Those who come from a Jewish background have one set of beliefs and behaviours; it is the fulfilment of all their hopes – Christianity is a natural development of their faith. For those from a non-Jewish background, it is completely new. There is plenty of room for misunderstanding and disagreement. Most of the letters are written to deal with specific situations where the churches or individuals are confused about some aspect of Christian teaching or are getting their behaviour wrong. In the letters we see the thinkers of the early Church wrestling under the guidance of the Holy Spirit with the significance of Jesus' life and death.

Of the 21 letters, 13 come from Paul. Some scholars have argued that he did not write all of them, but there are good reasons for accepting that he did. Paul gives us some of the most profound thinking and some of the most challenging practical instructions. Many of the letters are written to churches that he founded. The earliest are probably the two letters to the church in Thessalonica. They seem to be confused by the timing of Jesus' return. Some have given up work because they think that Jesus will be coming back any day. This may seem an attractive idea but Paul will have none of it – there is to be no sponging off others. His instructions here may be a challenge to one of the central planks of Roman society, the system where rich patrons would gather round them and support a number of 'clients'. The more clients, the greater the status of the patron. The **good news** can demand that we act in ways that cut across everything our society accepts as normal.

Others seem to have decided that Jesus isn't coming back because he hasn't done so already; an idea which seems to surface again in Paul's first letter to the church in Corinth (and also in Peter's second letter). Out of these struggles comes a better understanding of the future; Jesus is coming back and the whole of creation will be renewed.

The letter to the Galatians appears to have been written to a group of churches which Paul founded on his first missionary journey. They are being influenced by a group who were insisting that unless they kept all the details of the Jewish law, they could not be in a right relationship with God. Consequently, they were in danger of losing all the new freedom that they have in Jesus and going back to an old, unsatisfactory way of living. Paul uses some strong language to persuade them not to give up. It's not always easy to understand because he uses some complex illustrations from the Old Testament, but Galatians leaves us in no doubt that we are put right with God by faith and not by the things we do; that salvation is God's gift, not something we can earn. Using concepts that we may not find simple to grasp, Paul reminds them that Abraham was saved by faith in God and not by keeping the law.

Faith

Faith is a key idea throughout the Bible, but it comes to its fullest expression in Paul's writings. It is always through faith that we have a relationship with God – that was just as true for Abraham as it is for us (Romans 4:3). Faith is not just about believing certain facts, although when Paul speaks about 'the faith' (eg 1 Timothy 3:9) he often refers to the things that we believe; it is about committing ourselves to those things that we believe and, above all, committing ourselves to the God in whom we believe. Faith and trust are used to translate the same set of Greek words.

It is sometimes thought that Paul argues that in the Old Testament people were saved by keeping the law and, in the New Testament, by putting their trust in Jesus. In fact, his position is that people are only ever saved by trusting God. The law was given to show how those who had trusted God were to live, and to remind us that we cannot, in ourselves, do what God wants. The law could not bring us into a right relationship with God, but it can help us to live as God wants us to.

The fact that we are put right with God through faith does not mean that we can live as we want. In all his letters, Paul lays out the way that Christians should live. James wants us to understand that faith without works is useless (James

2:17,26). Although some have thought that Paul and James disagree, they are actually saying the same thing.

As we read the two letters to the Corinthians, it is a little like listening to one side of a conversation. In fact, many of the letters are like this – something that is worth remembering as we read them. The Corinthians had written to Paul with questions. He had heard about other things that were going on in the church. He writes to put them right on Church unity, sexual relationships, worship, and (again) Jesus' return. Some of his teaching seems strange to us – for example, the idea that women should always wear some head covering in churches. This reminds us that he was writing in a particular social and historical situation and we may have to do some digging to work out why he said some things and their significance for us today.

Romans is the fullest explanation of what God was doing in Jesus. If the Old Testament in its various ways points forward to Jesus, and the Gospels tell the story of his life and teaching, the letters, and supremely Romans, look back, reflecting on his life and death and what it all means for us. In Romans, Paul starts by establishing that all of us have failed to live as God wants, that as members of the human race we are all involved in the sin and rebellion which had its first expression in the Garden of Eden in Genesis 3. He then goes on to show how we can be put right with God through our faith, just as Abraham was. Abraham looked forward to what God was going to do (eg in Genesis 12:2,3); we look back, seeing what God has done, and put our trust in what he has accomplished through the death of Jesus. Paul explains how God dealt with sin; the Old Testament sacrifices dealt with sin in the past only because they were symbols of the death of Jesus and it is only with his death that sin is finally dealt with. The consequence is that we can live a new life in the power of the Spirit, knowing that we have a new relationship with God. In Romans, too, Paul deals with the question of where the Jews fit in to God's ongoing plan. In the concluding chapters, he gives us sound practical advice on how to live the Christian life.

Sacrifice

We are not far into the Bible before we encounter the idea of sacrifice. Possibly the first was the animal that provided the clothes for Adam and Eve (Genesis 3:21). We certainly have sacrifice in Genesis 4, with the offerings of Cain and Abel, and Noah offers God a sacrifice after the flood (Genesis 8:20). The lamb which was killed at the Passover and the elaborate instructions in Leviticus add to the Old Testament picture. There is considerable debate about the purpose of the sacrifices. Some seem to have been designed as an expression of a relationship (Leviticus 3) while others seem to have been designed to deal with sin (Leviticus 4). It appears that the sin was transferred to the animal and that in the death of the animal the serious nature of sin was recognised, a sense of remorse expressed and forgiveness obtained. Therefore, the life of the worshipper is redeemed through the offering of the animal. A price, or ransom, has been offered to obtain freedom.

These ideas are picked up in the New Testament, where Jesus is described as our Passover lamb (1 Corinthians 5:7), and a sacrifice (eg 1 John 2:2; 4:10); the Old Testament sacrifices point to Jesus and are fulfilled in him. A number of pictures are used to describe what this means. His death ensures that we are redeemed, we have been bought back, a price has been paid, our sin has been taken by him and we are now forgiven and freed. Sometimes this is described as the ransom price paid to buy our freedom. The language of atonement is often used; in the biblical languages this probably derives from the idea that our sins have been covered. One of the most sacred days in the Jewish calendar was the Day of Atonement (Leviticus 16) when the people confessed their sin and received God's forgiveness. Instead of facing God's just sentence, we now discover his gracious forgiveness.

Ephesians, Philippians and Colossians were written from prison. Probably they come from the period around AD 60 when Paul was under house arrest in Rome (Acts 28:30,31), but it is possible that they may come from an earlier period when he was in prison in Caesarea (Acts 23:23 – 25:12). They contain the result of mature reflection under the inspiration of the Spirit. There is clear teaching about who Jesus is and about what he has done for us. Philippians contains one of the best known brief descriptions of Jesus and his work:

> Your attitude should be the same as that of Christ Jesus:
> Who, being in very nature God,
>> did not consider equality with God something to be grasped,
> but made himself nothing,
>> taking the very nature of a servant,
>> being made in human likeness.
> And being found in appearance as a man,
>> he humbled himself
>> and became obedient to death – even death on a cross!
> Therefore God exalted him to the highest place
>> and gave him the name that is above every name,
> that at the name of Jesus every knee should bow,
>> in heaven and on earth and under the earth,
> and every tongue confess that Jesus Christ is Lord,
>> to the glory of God the Father.
>
> *Philippians 2:5–11*

At many points in these letters, we catch glimpses of Paul's deep love for the churches and his agony over things that go wrong. We see a man who is deeply committed to carrying out God's purposes in the world and who is determined to live for God, despite the opposition and pain that it often brings. This is part of the cost of following Jesus in a broken world. Just as in the Old Testament, here, too, we see that God is calling his people to be different and that is a costly business. The standards which Paul lays out are demanding, but he wants us to be motivated not by a sense of fear, but by a sense of gratitude. There is an interesting example of this in Paul's letter to Philemon, a church leader in Colosse, asking him to take back a runaway slave, Onesimus, on the grounds that they are brothers in Christ. This is an amazing challenge to the values of the time – the impact of Jesus is revolutionary.

As with Philemon, the remaining three letters of Paul are addressed to individuals, in this case to two of his associates who are now leading churches: Timothy in Ephesus and Titus in Crete. They were probably written towards the end of his life, possibly after release from an initial period of imprisonment in Rome and a brief period of further ministry before re-arrest and execution in the mid-60s. As well as giving plenty of personal encouragement, Paul describes how the church is to be organised and led. Christians differ on exactly how we are to apply the details but the key principles are that there should be structure and appointed leaders. The qualities Paul looks for in leaders are demanding in any age; leaders in the Church are to set an example of good behaviour.

That leaves the letters of James, Peter, John and Jude and the anonymous letter to the Hebrews. Hebrews is written to Jews who have become Christians and who are finding the going tough. They are in danger of giving up. The letter gives us some of the most detailed explanation of the way in which the Old Testament is a preparation for Jesus and helps us to see how everything fits together. The laws and the worship with its feasts, sacrifices and Temple are visual aids pointing forward. Now we have the reality, it would be foolish to go back; once we have arrived at the destination why would we return to the signposts? The writer spells out the dire consequences of giving up on Jesus (eg Hebrews 6:4–6).

James is rather different. Unlike the other letters, there is not much teaching in it; it is more like a collection of practical wisdom for living. The theme is a familiar one: God's people are meant to live in different ways from those around them. If we fail to do so, we are simply making it clear that our faith is not real. Some have suggested that James contradicts Paul's teaching that we are put right with God through **faith**. But there is no contradiction; they are coming from different angles and both agree that faith is the key, but it has to be worked out in practice.

Peter's letters are both addressed to a wide Christian audience.

He has similar concerns to those we have met before. He reminds his readers that they are a new, holy people as a result of the Jesus' death:

> But you are a chosen people, a royal priesthood, a holy nation, a people belonging to God, that you may declare the praises of him who called you out of darkness into his wonderful light. Once you were not a people, but now you are the people of God; once you had not received mercy, but now you have received mercy.
>
> *1 Peter 2:9,10*

These verses pick up Exodus 19:5,6 and Hosea 1:9 – 2:1; 2:23. God has only one plan which started way back and has now come into effect. Peter recognises that this makes demands on us and that living for Jesus won't always be easy. Many of those to whom he is writing are suffering for their **faith** and he encourages them to hang on, reminding them of the example of Jesus.

John's first letter, too, is addressed to a wider group of Christians. He wants to make sure that they believe the right things and do the right things. His great theme is love and he gives us the great summary of God's character, 'God is love' (1 John 4:8,16); but if God loves us, then we must love one another. His second and third letters are probably addressed to individual Christians and deal with the same twin themes of truth and love.

Jude reminds us again that we live in a messed up world and that it is hard not to be drawn into its way of living. He concludes with a great note of praise to God who can help us to stand firm until the day that Jesus returns (Jude 24,25).

We now have almost the complete picture. We have seen the promise of the Old Testament, come to its fulfilment in Jesus, and have seen what that means. To summarise, God has made a good world and we have lost our relationship with him and messed up the world through our selfishness and determination to go our way rather than his. From the very start, God has been determined to put that right and planned to do so through entering into the world of humans and giving himself in the person of Jesus to take the penalty for sin, demonstrate his love for us despite our failure, and destroy the power of sin and death in our lives. We now have the opportunity, if we place our trust in him, to become the children of God and live new lives in the power of the Spirit. We are called to live in distinctive ways, but we are not required to do it in our own strength. As the people of God, we share in his mission to call the people of all nations to join us in that new relationship with him. We see that God's goal for the world is not just about our own individual relationship with him, but about something far bigger; which leads us to our final chapter.

New world coming

Remember our 'view from outer space'? We saw that the Bible looked like four large land masses or 'continents': the creation of the world, the spoiling of the world through sin, the sorting out of sin through Jesus and the re-creation of the world (see p11,12). Zooming in, we can take a closer look at what is going to happen. The Bible book that has most to say about this is Revelation, but it is a theme we find throughout the Bible.

To our way of thinking, Revelation seems a strange book. If anything, it looks a bit like a sci-fi fantasy, with strange images, dream sequences and odd characters. Everything seems fluid. This is the language of poetry and if we try to take it too literally we shall miss the point. It is the broad sweep that matters, not trying to make sense of all the details. This type of writing was not uncommon at the time, and has been given a special name, apocalyptic, from the Greek word meaning an unveiling. We also find it in the second half of Daniel and in much of Zechariah.

In the Old Testament we have hints of what God is going to do. We have seen how it looks forward to the establishment of the **kingdom** – the time when God will come and rule his people himself:

> My dwelling-place will be with them; I will be their God, and they will be my people.
> *Ezekiel 37:27*

Often this is described in very physical terms, sometimes in terms of a new creation:

> 'Behold, I will create
>> new heavens and a new earth.
> The former things will not be remembered,
>> nor will they come to mind.
>
> ...
>
> The wolf and the lamb will feed together,
>> and the lion will eat straw like the ox,
>> but dust will be the serpent's food.
> They will neither harm nor destroy
>> on all my holy mountain,'
>>>> says the LORD.

Isaiah 65:17,25

Jesus talks of a time when the Son of Man (a term he uses of himself) would return, coming in power and great glory (Mark 13:26). As we have seen, the letters use similar language, emphasising Jesus' return:

> For the Lord himself will come down from heaven, with a loud command, with the voice of the archangel and with the trumpet call of God, and the dead in Christ will rise first. After that, we who are still alive and are left will be caught up together with them in the clouds to meet the Lord in the air. And so we will be with the Lord for ever.

1 Thessalonians 4:16,17

And pointing to a renewed and restored creation:

> That day will bring about the destruction of the heavens by fire, and the elements will melt in the heat. But in keeping with his promise we are looking forward to a new heaven and a new earth, the home of righteousness.

2 Peter 3:12,13

So by the time we come to Revelation, we are prepared. In fact, Revelation frequently quotes from and alludes to the Old Testament. What seems to be something new is in fact part of the same overall picture that we have been looking at.

Revelation takes the form of a circular letter addressed to seven churches in Asia Minor – the western end of Turkey. The first three chapters contain specific messages to these churches but they don't stop there; the book should be seen as a whole and the letters provide an important clue to understanding it. Revelation deals with specific issues at the end of the first century. These small churches are facing fierce persecution. We cannot be certain exactly what form it took but there were many local outbreaks of persecution in the first century and two wider attacks on the Church, the first under Emperor Nero in the mid sixties, and the second under the Emperor Domitian in the nineties. It is likely that both Peter and Paul were executed during the first. Revelation was written during the second to encourage these struggling Christians, telling them that God is in control and he is working out his purposes even if it doesn't seem like it. The symbols and pictures that we may find hard to understand would have made sense to the first readers.

Some have argued that all the symbols are describing things that had happened or were happening at the time; it is describing recent history. Others have seen it as describing only the things that will happen at the end of time. A third approach has been to see it as describing the ways things are at all points in history. There is probably truth in all of these. The first readers needed to know that God was active in the affairs of their world. So 'Babylon', described as a prostitute riding a beast with seven heads and, we are told, having seven hills (Revelation 17:3–11), is almost certainly code for Rome, which was built around seven hills. When they read of the destruction of 'Babylon' in chapter 18 they could draw comfort and strength from the reminder that God would destroy the power of the apparently invincible Rome. Similarly, we can draw comfort and strength in our time, when we see the church struggling and persecuted and evil apparently winning, from the knowledge that God will ultimately destroy all such oppressors at whatever point in history they appear; their power is limited and his is not. Looking to the future, we can know that all human empires will be finally swept away and all things will be renewed.

The picture that emerges is of a God who is in control and who is working out all things according to his plan. The last two chapters describe his final victory over evil and the establishment of his new world, in which he is with his people, and peace and justice reign.

> Then I saw a new heaven and a new earth, for the first heaven and the first earth had passed away, and there was no longer any sea. I saw the Holy City, the new Jerusalem, coming down out of heaven from God, prepared as a bride beautifully dressed for her husband. And I heard a loud voice from the throne saying, 'Now the dwelling of God is with men, and he will live with them. They will be his people, and God himself will be with them and be their God. He will wipe every tear from their eyes. There will be no more death or mourning or crying or pain, for the old order of things has passed away.'
>
> *Revelation 21:1–4*

Key to our understanding of Revelation and the future that God has, is the figure of 'a Lamb, slaughtered but standing tall' (Revelation 5:6, *The Message*). Jesus, to whom the sacrificial system of the Old Testament points, is at the centre of God's future for the world. He is the key to making sense of the Bible, the unifying factor who brings it all together. All of the Bible bears witness to God's great plan to save humanity and restore creation through his life, death and resurrection.

We are ultimately heading, not to some vague 'heaven' as it is so often depicted, or to a place of disembodied spirits. The vision that we're given is of real, earthy stuff, inhabited by real bodies. The Christian hope, which is not some vague idea but a certain conviction that all will be well, is not of going to heaven when we die, but of resurrection with a new body inhabiting a new earth. This may not seem easy to imagine, but it does suggest a more glorious future than we could ever imagine. This is the goal of all that God has been doing, this is his plan and purpose for the world, this is what the big picture looks like.

GROUND LEVEL

Exploring the detail

We are now down at ground level and can see only our immediate surroundings, in this case individual books, or possibly even sections of books. Although it can be helpful to see the Bible as a library with 66 books in it, this can hide the fact that it tells one story, and that God has given us one connected book which he intends us to see in that way. Each book of the Bible has its place within the whole.

We are about to take a very brief look at each individual book, but there are some questions we shall not be able to answer. In the case of some books we know a lot about the background, but for others we know very little because the Bible does not give us the information. This need not worry us. Most of the important things are clear and, where we don't have all the answers, we can trust the God who inspired the writing of each part of the whole. One of the amazing things is, in fact, the way in which the Bible, written over a period of over a thousand years, holds together and points in the same direction.

While it is useful to know something about the background to help us understand *what* the book is about and *how* we should understand it, it is possible to become so obsessed with some of these details that we can miss out on what God is saying. The important thing is to listen to God and then to respond with obedience.

Sometimes, sorting out what God is saying will be hard; it will seem like pressing on through what seems like darkness in order to reach the light. There is nothing wrong with that; the greatest treasures often require the greatest effort to discover. Nevertheless, if we approach the Bible in the right way we will find that its truth shines out more brightly. Some practical things may help us here.

We need the Holy Spirit to open our eyes and help us to see what God is saying. If we start with our minds and our wisdom we will be putting a barrier in the way. So, whenever we come to the Bible, we must ask God to help us to understand

We can draw on the wisdom of others. In nearly two thousand years of Church history, many have thought deeply about the meaning of the Bible. We can benefit from the work they have done. There are many scholars today who have the benefit of new archaeological discoveries and research and the fruits of their work are available to us in commentaries and dictionaries. There are others in our churches or fellowships who are reading the Bible, and talking to them may open up new insights. If we hit a passage that seems especially difficult, it is always worth finding someone else to talk to or a book to consult.

If we go back to our original picture, we have seen that there are different sorts of terrain in the landscape. Looking at the world, there are hills and mountains, streams and valleys, meadows and forests, narrow city streets and wide open stretches of moorland – to say nothing of the vast expanse of the oceans. Each of these requires a different approach and may need different clothing or equipment. A five-minute stroll along the beach on a sunny day needs no special preparation, but a seven-day hike along a long-distance path involving long periods above 1,000 metres will require both good preparation and the right gear.

The Bible works in a similar way. As we look at the individual parts more closely, we shall find that understanding the history and the poetry, the letters and the laws, the prophecy and the parables will require different preparation and different approaches.

Another thing to remember is that we always come to the Bible with our own experiences and background. Those raised in poverty will read verses differently from those with a wealthy upbringing; those from stable families differently from those who come from less happy homes. Being aware of this will help us spot places where we might miss the point or misunderstand because of our own experience or perspective. But we shouldn't worry too much because, if we are open and ask God to help us as we read, we shall find that these things affect our understanding less as the Bible does its work in our lives.

We read the Bible to get to know God better, to love him more, to live as he wants us to live and to understand more about his character and his plans for the world. So, with that in mind, let's prepare to look at some of the detail. This probably isn't a section to read through from beginning to end (unless of course you want to) but one to refer to when you need the information.

Genesis

Who wrote it? Much of the material probably comes from Moses but has been revised by later editors.

When? The original material sometime between 1300 and 1250 BC.

What's in it? Creation, human disobedience and its consequences, God's promise to do something about it, the lives of Noah, Abraham, Isaac, Jacob and Joseph showing God at work.

Where does it fit? Tells us that God made the world, that human selfishness messed it up and that God has a plan to put it right.

Exodus

Who wrote it? Much of the material probably comes from Moses but has been revised by later editors.

When? Probably sometime between 1300 and 1250 BC.

What's in it? God delivers his people from Egypt, gives them laws about how they are to live in relationship with him and with one another, and leads them towards the new land he has for them.

Where does it fit? Sets the pattern for God's saving activity. The exodus from Egypt is a foreshadowing of God's greater deliverance of all humanity from sin. The law and the regulations for worship show us a holy God who enters into relationship with his people but expects them to live in distinctive ways.

Leviticus

Who wrote it? Most of the material was given to Moses by God on Mount Sinai.

When? Probably sometime around 1280 BC.

What's in it? Laws about living in community and staying in right relationship with God.

Where does it fit? The sacrificial system reminds us that God is holy and that we can only be right with him when sin is dealt with through sacrifice, pointing us forward to the sacrifice of Jesus.

Numbers

Who wrote it? Much of the material probably comes from Moses but has been revised by later editors.

When? Probably sometime between 1300 and 1250 BC.

What's in it? Israel's journey to their new land, their lack of trust when they get there and 40 years more in the wilderness.

Where does it fit? God moving forward his purposes for Abraham's descendants to be established in their own land, but also showing again the consequence of human failure.

Deuteronomy

Who wrote it? Much of the material probably comes from Moses but has been revised by later editors.

When? Probably sometime between 1300 and 1250 BC.

What's in it? Moses' final words to the people before they enter the land. He reminds them of all that God has done and encourages them to remain faithful.

Where does it fit? God moving forward his purposes for Abraham's descendants by taking them from Egypt, making them a people, and entering into a covenant with them in which he promises to care for them and requires them to be faithful to him.

Joshua

Who wrote it? We don't know. Much of it goes back to contemporary records, some from Joshua himself, but it was revised later.

When? Sources dating from around 1200 BC, put together later.

What's in it? Moses' successor Joshua (whose name means 'The Lord saves') leads the people across the River Jordan into the land, winning several battles.

Where does it fit? Abraham's descendants now have a permanent home. This is seen in the New Testament as a picture of the permanent relationship which we have with God through Jesus (the Greek form of Joshua).

Judges

Who wrote it? We don't know, but much of it goes back to contemporary records.

When? Original sources date from the period around 1200–1000 BC. We don't know when it took its present form.

What's in it? Once in the land the people forget what God has done and start to worship the gods that the people of the land worship. God calls them back through allowing them to fall under the control of neighbouring powers and, when they repent, saving them through leaders known as judges.

Where does it fit? God does not give up on people even when they choose to go their own way.

Ruth

Who wrote it? We don't know.

When? We can't be sure, but the action takes place in the period of the judges.

What's in it? Naomi returns to Israel from Moab (where she had gone to escape a famine) with her widowed daughter-in-law Ruth, who, although from a different nation, chooses to remain faithful to Naomi. In Israel, Ruth finds a new husband, Boaz.

Where does it fit? Boaz is in a special relationship to Naomi and takes the role of what was called the 'kinsman-redeemer'. This becomes a picture of the way in which God redeems his people and enters into a relationship with them. Ruth is the great-grandmother of King David and thus features as one of Jesus' ancestors.

1 and 2 Samuel

Who wrote it? We don't know.

When? We can't be sure when it took its present form but the action takes place in the period around 1100–970 BC and much of the material in its original form dates from then.

What's in it? Israel move from being led by judges to having a king. The first king, Saul, and his successor, David, secure the land against hostile neighbours. Much of 2 Samuel is taken up with the family affairs of David who failed badly, committing adultery and murder, but is still seen as a good king who follows God.

Where does it fit? In demanding a king the people rejected God as King, but God rules through the kings and they become forerunners of the king God will one day send and who will rule for him in a new way.

1 and 2 Kings

Who wrote it? We don't know.

When? We can't be sure when it took its present form but the action takes place in the period around 970–580 BC and much of the material in its original form dates from then.

What's in it? The reign of David's son Solomon, after whose death the kingdom splits into two. There is then a succession of kings, both good and bad. In the northern half (now called Israel) they are mostly bad and lead the people away from God until the north is conquered by Assyria in 722 BC and disappears from history. The south (called Judah) continues with a similar cycle of good and bad kings until Jerusalem falls to the Babylonians in 587 BC and many of the people are taken into exile in Babylon.

Where does it fit? Tells the story of the continuing failure of God's people to live as he wants and to show his power and glory in the world, and thus demonstrating the need for God to act in a new way.

1 and 2 Chronicles

Who wrote it? We can't be certain.

When? Probably compiled in the fifth or fourth centuries BC.

What's in it? It covers the same historical period as Kings but concentrates on the southern kingdom after the split and is especially interested in aspects of worship.

Where does it fit? Describes the struggles and ultimate failure of God's people, and emphasises the importance of sincere worship and obedient trust.

Ezra

Who wrote it? We don't know, but it seems to be a continuation of Chronicles.

When? Probably compiled in the fifth or fourth centuries BC.

What's in it? Tells the story of the return from Babylon in 535 BC, of the rebuilding of the Temple and of Ezra's visit in 458 BC.

Where does it fit? The return from exile shows God's continuing purposes for his people and points to what Jesus will later do in bringing people back from spiritual exile. Babylon becomes a symbol for evil that will be defeated.

Nehemiah

Who wrote it? We don't know, but it seems to be a continuation of Chronicles and Ezra.

When? Probably compiled in the fifth or fourth centuries BC.

What's in it? Nehemiah's arrival in Jerusalem in 445 BC, the rebuilding of the walls, and a challenge to live as God wants.

Where does it fit? Demonstrates God's ongoing commitment to fulfil his promises to bless the world through Abraham's descendants, and the importance of living in the right way.

Esther

Who wrote it? We don't know.

When? Probably between 450 and 400 BC.

What's in it? The story of how Esther becomes wife of King Xerxes of Persia and foils a plot to wipe out the Jews in exile.

Where does it fit? Shows God's protection of his people, and thus of his ultimate purposes for them and for the world, even in dark times.

Job

Who wrote it? We don't know.

When? We can't be sure – suggestions vary from 970–250 BC.

What's in it? Job loses everything and the book is a dialogue between him and various friends about the causes of suffering. Job's plea that he is innocent of any sin which might have caused it and his request that God might intervene is finally answered when God speaks. God does not explain the causes of Job's suffering but demonstrates that he is in control. Earlier in the book, we have been shown that Satan is responsible for Job's suffering but that his power is limited by God.

Where does it fit? It shows something of the struggle of living as humans in a broken world, demonstrating that only God can provide any final answer to the suffering. There are hints that one day he will do this in ways that Job and his friends cannot understand at the time, but which he does through the death and resurrection of Jesus.

Psalms

Who wrote it? Various writers – many are attributed to David and there is no good reason to doubt this.

When? Individual psalms were probably composed in the period from 1070 to around 400 BC.

What's in it? The psalms take a variety of forms. There are songs of thanksgiving and praise and anguished cries to God for justice; some express individual concerns and others are written on behalf of the community. They later became central to the worship of Israel.

Where does it fit? Psalms gives an insight into the joys and fears, hopes and pain of a worshipping community. It says much about how we can relate to God in all sorts of circumstances. Several of the psalms, including some written for the king, look forward to a coming king who will reign in a new way. The New Testament sees these as relating to Jesus who comes as our King. Some, like Psalm 22, anticipate his pain and suffering.

Proverbs

Who wrote it? Various writers, with a significant proportion coming from Solomon.

When? Probably mostly around 950 BC.

What's in it? A collection of pithy, down-to-earth practical advice for, and observations of, daily living.

Where does it fit? It reminds us that all wisdom originates in God. In chapter 8, wisdom is personified and this is often seen as a reference to Jesus who comes to us as God's wisdom.

Ecclesiastes

Who wrote it? The book claims to have been written by a son of David, king in Jerusalem, and this has often been taken to mean it must have been written by Solomon. The contents would certainly fit, but the language comes from a later date, so if it goes back to Solomon it was revised later.

When? If it goes back to Solomon, around 950 BC.

What's in it? A man's failure to find satisfaction in the pleasures of life, leading to the conclusion that true satisfaction can only be found in God.

Where does it fit? A reminder that the true purpose of our lives can only be found in doing things God's way.

Song of Songs

Who wrote it? Traditionally thought to be Solomon and, although the references to him do not necessarily mean that it was written by him, it is a possibility.

When? Around 950 BC.

What's in it? Explicit and graphic love poems.

Where does it fit? Although many have seen it as an expression of the love between God and his people or between Christ and his Church, it starts out as an expression of the value of human love, reminding us that the whole of life is lived out in the presence of God. Given the marriage imagery that is used of God and his people, it is reasonable to see a secondary spiritual sense.

Isaiah

Who wrote it? The book is the recorded prophecies of Isaiah. Many scholars have thought that chapters 40–66 come from a different later prophet, but there are good reasons to see the book as a single unit which originates from Isaiah, although chapters 40–66 relate to a later period than chapters 1–39.

When? Isaiah prophesied from about 740 to about 700 BC.

What's in it? Chapters 1–35 are a succession of challenges to Judah (the southern kingdom after the split) to stop worshipping idols and oppressing the poor and come back to God, with warnings of judgement if they do not. There are also some messages directed to surrounding nations. Chapters 36–39 are a historical account of an invasion by the Assyrians also recorded in 2 Kings 18,19 and 2 Chronicles 32. Chapters 40–55 are words of hope directed to the Israelites promising that God will bring them back from exile. Chapters 56–66 are words of encouragement directed to the exiles who have returned.

Where does it fit? Like many of the prophets, Isaiah wrestles with the failure of God's people, but sees hope beyond the failure. Isaiah 40–55 contain a number of references to the servant including a very well-known passage in Isaiah 53 which looks forward to the coming of Jesus and his death for us.

Jeremiah

Who wrote it? These are the recorded prophecies of Jeremiah.

When? Jeremiah was active from about 626 BC to the fall of Jerusalem in 587 BC.

What's in it? A call to Judah to come back to God, whom they have forsaken, with warnings of judgement if they do not. Jeremiah struggles with the message. He also meets opposition from the authorities and his peers. But, like Isaiah, he can see beyond the present difficulties to a time when God will make a new covenant with his people.

Where does it fit? Jeremiah looks forward to a new covenant which God will make with his people, giving them a new inner motivation to obey him.

Lamentations

Who wrote it? It is anonymous although often attributed to Jeremiah, probably through a similarity of feeling.

When? Sometime soon after the fall of Jerusalem in 587 BC.

What's in it? A series of laments about the fall of Jerusalem and the disgrace of God's people.

Where does it fit? It shows that when God's people fail, God's reputation suffers, but his love remains constant. If God is to establish his reputation in the world and show his love for his people, he will have to do something new for them.

Ezekiel

Who wrote it? Ezekiel.

When? Ezekiel was active from about 593 BC, when he was probably among the first wave of exiles taken to Babylon, to about 570 BC.

What's in it? Some strange language and imagery, the first part of the book being mostly warnings about the people's failure. After some prophecies about foreign nations (chapters 25–32), Ezekiel looks ahead to God's future restoration of Israel. These chapters include the vision of a valley of dry bones which God brings to life and the vision of the restored Temple.

Where does it fit? While these prophecies of the future are partly fulfilled when Israel returns from exile, they are only completely fulfilled when Jesus comes. Some of them look still further forward to the return of Jesus and the restored creation.

Daniel

Who wrote it? Chapters 1–6 are historical and speak of Daniel in the third person. In chapters 7–12 Daniel speaks in the first person. So either two earlier sources were brought together or Daniel uses the literary device of the third person in the earlier chapters.

When? Many modern scholars have argued that Daniel must have been written in the second century because of its knowledge of later history, but that assumes that God cannot give insights into the future. There are good reasons for taking the book at face value and seeing it as originating in Babylon in the sixth century BC.

What's in it? An account of Daniel's life in captivity in Babylon and how, through his God-given wisdom and ability to interpret dreams, he rises to a position of power. In chapters 7–12 we have an account of Daniel's visions of the future, often written in strange language with unusual images.

Where does it fit? It reminds us that God protects his people and will ensure that his plans for the world will be achieved. This ultimately happens when Jesus introduces an unshakeable kingdom unlike the passing kingdoms of the world. These chapters have different levels of fulfilment: in the second century, in the coming of Jesus and the fall of Jerusalem (again) in AD 70, and in Jesus' return at the end of time.

Hosea

Who wrote it? Hosea.

When? Around 755–722 BC.

What's in it? Hosea prophesied in the northern kingdom. His prophecies are a call to return to God, who never gives up on his people. This is powerfully modelled by Hosea's own loving faithfulness in marriage to an unfaithful prostitute.

Where does it fit? Reminds us that God will never finally give up on his people. Hosea has a strong emphasis on God's steadfast or covenant love, which is supremely shown in Jesus. Matthew sees Hosea's words about a son being called from Egypt as having fulfilment in Jesus.

Joel

Who wrote it? Joel.

When? It is hard to be certain but possibly 515–500 BC.

What's in it? Joel sees a plague of locusts as a call to return to God.

Where does it fit? The 'day of the Lord' is a key idea in Joel (1:15; 2:31; 3:14). His contemporaries see this as a day when God would come and give his people victory. Joel sees it as a day of both judgement and opportunity. In the New Testament, Jesus' coming is seen as a partial realisation of the day of the Lord, with his second coming as another level of fulfilment. Joel also sees it as a time when the Spirit will be poured out; Peter sees this as being fulfilled at Pentecost.

Amos

Who wrote it? Amos.

When? Probably about 760 BC.

What's in it? Amos was active in the northern kingdom of Israel at a time of great prosperity but of great injustice. God will act to bring judgement if the rich do not stop oppressing the poor and if the people do not live by God's standards.

Where does it fit? For Amos, as for Joel, the 'day of the Lord' is a key theme (5:18). While for his contemporaries it is the longed-for day when God would defeat their enemies, for him it is a time of judgement rather than victory for Israel, a time when God will come to bring about justice. This is ultimately fulfilled in Jesus; in his earthly life when God's just rule is established, and in his return when it will be seen and experienced by all.

Obadiah

Who wrote it? Obadiah.

When? We cannot be certain, but the evidence may suggest a time shortly after the fall of Jerusalem in 587 BC.

What's in it? Prophecies against Edom for their opposition to Judah.

Where does it fit? The concluding verse reminds us that God will establish his universal rule over all the earth.

Jonah

Who wrote it? Jonah is the hero rather than the author; we can't be sure who wrote it.

When? The action probably takes place at some time between 800 and 750 BC but the book may have been written later.

What's in it? God calls Jonah to go to Nineveh, but Jonah refuses. God gets him there in the end to preach a message of forgiveness. Jonah is upset when Nineveh repents and God has to show him that his grace is for all.

Where does it fit? God's grace and forgiveness are for all people. Jesus uses the book as a sign, picking up the idea of Jonah's three days in the fish as a parallel to his own three days in the tomb (eg Matthew 12:39,40). In doing so, he is pointing out that in him God's grace and forgiveness are offered to all.

Micah

Who wrote it? Micah.

When? Micah was active in Judah from about 740 BC to about 687 BC.

What's in it? Micah denounces the injustices of Judah and Israel and tells of judgement if they do not change their ways. But beyond the judgement he sees restoration.

Where does it fit? Micah looks forward to a time of universal peace when all will worship God. He sees this being established through a ruler who would come from Bethlehem. Matthew 2:3–6 tells us that the Jewish leaders saw this as a prophecy of the Messiah.

Nahum

Who wrote it? Nahum.

When? Shortly before Nineveh, the capital of Assyria, fell in 612 BC.

What's in it? A fierce attack on Assyria for its cruelty.

Where does it fit? No one can escape God's just judgement.

Habakkuk

Who wrote it? Habakkuk.

When? Sometime between the Babylonian conquest of Assyria in 612 BC and the fall of Jerusalem to the Babylonians in 587 BC.

What's in it? Habakkuk's debate with God about the way God seems to be ignoring injustice.

Where does it fit? Demonstrates that God is always in control and is always just, even when we do not understand. In a key verse (Habakkuk 2:4) Habakkuk explains that it is our faith that puts us right with God, a verse that is quoted by Paul (Romans 1:17; Galatians 3:11) and in Hebrews 10:38.

Zephaniah

Who wrote it? Zephaniah.

When? Sometime between 640 BC and 612 BC.

What's in it? Prophecies of judgement against Judah. The day of the Lord features strongly, seen as a day of judgement, but beyond judgement there is hope.

Where does it fit? Although the hope is initially realised in the return from exile, it has its full expression only in Jesus when he comes to draw people back to God.

Haggai

Who wrote it? Haggai.

When? 520 BC.

What's in it? Encouragement to the returned exiles to build the Temple.

Where does it fit? As an encouragement to put God first and to give worship its proper place in our lives, it prepares the way for Jesus who enables us to worship God correctly. Hebrews sees Haggai's word about a shaking associated with the coming of the 'desired of all nations' as a prediction of the eternal kingdom that Jesus will establish and that can never be shaken (Haggai 2:6, see Hebrews 12:26,27).

Zechariah

Who wrote it? Zechariah.

When? About 520 BC.

What's in it? Encouragements to build the Temple, and promises of a secure future for God's people in the form of visions which are not always easy to understand.

Where does it fit? Zechariah's promise of a coming king who will ride on donkey and of a good shepherd who will be sold for 30 shekels of silver, as a result of which the flock will be scattered, are all fulfilled in Jesus.

Malachi

Who wrote it? Malachi.

When? About 450 BC.

What's in it? A call to be serious about worshipping God.

Where does it fit? As the last book in the Old Testament, with still 400 years to run before Jesus, Malachi continues to prepare the way. He talks of one who will bring healing and of the messenger who will come to the Temple like refiner's fire.

Matthew

Who wrote it? The Gospel is anonymous but there are good early traditions suggesting that Matthew was the author.

When? We can't be sure exactly but probably between AD 60 and AD 80.

What's in it? The birth, life, death and resurrection of Jesus. Matthew records more of Jesus' teaching than Mark or Luke and has a special interest in the fulfilment of Old Testament prophecy, Jesus as King and the kingdom, and the Church fulfilling Israel's calling to be a holy people and to show God to the world.

Where does it fit? In Jesus, God's plan is carried out. The last week of Jesus' life occupies over a third of the book, showing how important Jesus' death is in God's plan to save the world.

Mark

Who wrote it? It is anonymous but a strong early tradition names Mark, the companion of Paul and cousin of Barnabas, as the author. The tradition also claims that he got his material from Peter.

When? Probably AD 60–70.

What's in it? The ministry, death and resurrection of Jesus. Mark is the most concise of the Gospels and the action moves at a rapid pace.

Where does it fit? In Jesus, God's plan comes about. The last week of Jesus' life occupies over a third of the book, showing how important Jesus' death is in God's plan to save the world.

Luke

Who wrote it? It is anonymous but the early tradition is that Luke, a doctor who travelled with Paul on some of his journeys, wrote both this and Acts. Not an eyewitness, he tells that he took great care in collecting his material.

When? Probably AD 62–70.

What's in it? The birth, life, death and resurrection of Jesus. Luke seems to write for Gentiles and has a particular interest in the poor and in women.

Where does it fit? In Jesus, God's plan is realised. While Luke does not give as much space to the last week of Jesus' earthly life as Mark and Matthew, it still takes up a significant part.

John

Who wrote it? The Gospel states that it is written by the beloved apostle normally thought to have been John.

When? Generally thought to have been the last Gospel to be written, probably about AD 90.

What's in it? The life, ministry and death of Jesus. John's emphases include light and darkness, life and death. He includes longer sections of teaching than any of the other Gospels.

Where does it fit? In Jesus, God's plan is realised. John includes several hints about Old Testament fulfilment. The grace of God revealed in Jesus does what the law could not do. John gives even more space than Matthew and Mark to the last week of Jesus' earthly life and includes a long section of Jesus' teaching at the Last Supper. He has a strong emphasis on Jesus as Messiah and Son of God.

Acts

Who wrote it? Luke, as a continuation of his Gospel.

When? Possibly around AD 63–65.

What's in it? The spread of the early Church from the years immediately after the death of Jesus to Paul's imprisonment in Rome in the early sixties. Paul's journeys take up a large part of the book.

Where does it fit? Now that God has come in Jesus and has acted to bring salvation to all, the news must be told in obedience to Jesus' command. The Holy Spirit, promised by Jesus and foretold by Ezekiel and Joel, gives the early Church the power to travel with the good news of what God has done. The promise to Abraham that the nations will be blessed is being fulfilled.

Romans

Who wrote it? Paul.

When? About AD 57.

What's in it? A full explanation of all that God has done for us in Jesus, who gave his life to save sinful men and women and give them new life, and a encouragement to live that new, distinctive life in the power of the Spirit.

Where does it fit? Looking back to what God has done in Jesus and making sense of it in our present as we discover what it means to be and to live as the people of God.

1 Corinthians

Who wrote it? Paul.

When? AD 53–54.

What's in it? Paul deals with a number of issues in the life of the Corinthian church, including division, immorality, marriage, disorderly worship and questions about the resurrection.

Where does it fit? Working out what it means to live as the people of God, saved through the death Jesus and filled with the Spirit but living in a confused and broken world.

2 Corinthians

Who wrote it? Paul.

When? About AD 55.

What's in it? Paul's defence of his calling to be an apostle in the face of criticism from the Corinthians. In a very personal letter, he shows how the glory of Christ is at work in his people and how our weakness can be a way for God's power to be shown.

Where does it fit? Working out what it means to be servants of Jesus, proclaiming the message of what God has done.

Galatians

Who wrote it? Paul.

When? Probably AD 48 or 49.

What's in it? Paul strongly encourages the Galatians not to abandon their Christian faith and makes it clear that we can only be put right with God through faith in Jesus and can only live as God wants in the power of the Spirit.

Where does it fit? Explains how Jesus' life, death and resurrection bring us a new relationship with God and enables us to live in the power of the Spirit.

Ephesians

Who wrote it? Paul (although this is often disputed).

When? Paul writes in captivity so probably from Rome which would give a date of about AD 61. It may have been written earlier (about AD 58) if the captivity referred to is in Caesarea.

What's in it? An explanation of what God has done for us in Jesus and of his ongoing purpose for the Church, with a challenge to live lives worthy of him.

Where does it fit? Explains the significance of Jesus' life, death and resurrection for our life and mission as the people of God.

Philippians

Who wrote it? Paul.

When? Paul writes in captivity so probably from Rome which would give a date of about AD 61. It may have been written earlier (about AD 58) if the captivity referred to is in Caesarea.

What's in it? A challenge to focus our attention on Jesus and to become like him in the way that we live. Philippians includes some of the clearest and most inspiring teaching about who Jesus is and what he did.

Where does it fit? Explains the significance of Jesus' life, death and resurrection – especially, what it means for our attitudes and lifestyle.

Colossians

Who wrote it? Paul.

When? Paul writes in captivity so probably from Rome which would give a date of about AD 61. It may have been written earlier (about AD 58) if the captivity referred to is in Caesarea.

What's in it? Warnings to avoid certain false teachings and to keep our attention fixed on Jesus while living as he would want us to.

Where does it fit? Explains the significance of Jesus' life, death and resurrection and lays the foundations for a Christian worldview in the face of alternative ideas.

1 and 2 Thessalonians

Who wrote it? Paul.

When? Both letters written within a few months of each other around AD 50.

What's in it? Both are personal letters in which Paul reviews his relationship with the church. His main reason for writing seems to be to encourage them and to put right certain ideas about Jesus' return.

Where does it fit? Working out how we are to live as we wait for the return of Jesus.

1 and 2 Timothy

Who wrote it? Paul (but this has been disputed).

When? 1 Timothy probably during a brief period of freedom about which we have no other information following Paul's captivity in Rome; so about AD 64 or 65, and 2 Timothy from prison facing trial and execution so about AD 66 or 67.

What's in it? Paul writes to encourage the young Timothy in his leadership of the church in Ephesus, explaining how the church should be organised at a practical level, outlining the qualities for leadership.

Where does it fit? Working out the mission of the Church, as it is called to witness to what God has done in Jesus.

Titus

Who wrote it? Paul (but this has been disputed).

When? Probably during a brief period of freedom about which we have no other information following his captivity in Rome; so about AD 64 or 65.

What's in it? Instruction to Titus leading the church in Crete about church order, the importance of right belief and correct behaviour.

Where does it fit? Working out the mission of the Church, as it is called to witness to what God has done in Jesus.

Philemon

Who wrote it? Paul.

When? Probably from captivity in Rome about AD 61.

What's in it? A request for Philemon, a church leader in Colosse, to take back a runaway slave, Onesimus, and recognise him as a brother in Christ.

Where does it fit? Working out the practical implications of living as people who have put our trust in Jesus.

Hebrews

Who wrote it? We don't know.

When? Probably between AD 64 and AD 70.

What's in it? An encouragement to Jews who had put their trust in Jesus not to turn away from him. The argument is based on Jesus as the fulfilment of all that the Old Testament had foreshadowed in the sacrifices, the priesthood and the worship in the Temple.

Where does it fit? Gives us the fullest explanation of the way in which the Old Testament speaks about Jesus, but not an easy read.

James

Who wrote it? James, the brother of Jesus and leader of the Jerusalem church.

When? Possibly around AD 50.

What's in it? Practical instruction on living the Christian life with an emphasis on the necessity of demonstrating our faith in changed behaviour; there are many similarities to the teaching of Jesus.

Where does it fit? Working out the practical implications of living as the people of God after the death and resurrection of Jesus.

1 and 2 Peter

Who wrote it? Both claim to be by Peter and, while some have questioned this particularly in the case of 2 Peter, there are good grounds for accepting this.

When? Sometime around AD 62–63.

What's in it? 1 Peter is an encouragement to Christians to stand firm in the face of opposition and false accusation, bearing in mind the example of Jesus and the reality of their salvation; 2 Peter is an encouragement to hold to true belief and right behaviour in the face of temptation.

Where does it fit? Working out how to live as followers of Jesus, God's new people, in the face of hostility.

1 John

Who wrote it? The letter is anonymous, but the style and the content make the early tradition that they were by John highly likely.

When? We cannot be sure, but possibly around AD 90.

What's in it? A strong emphasis on the need to hold to the truth in the face of false teaching, and to love one another.

Where does it fit? Working out how to stand for the truth of who Jesus is and what he did, while also showing the sort of love that God is and that Jesus demonstrated.

2 and 3 John

Who wrote it? The letters are anonymous, but the style and the content make the early tradition that they were by John highly likely.

When? We cannot be sure, but possibly around AD 90.

What's in it? Both are short personal letters with similar sentiments to 1 John.

Where does it fit? Working out how to stand for the truth about Jesus and guarding against error – but doing so in a way that shows love.

Jude

Who wrote it? Jude, the brother of James and, therefore, of Jesus.

When? It is hard to be sure but probably between AD 70 and AD 90.

What's in it? A fierce attack on false teaching, especially that which leads to wrong behaviour.

Where does it fit? Emphasises the need to hold firm to the truth of what God has done in Jesus.

Revelation

Who wrote it? John, probably the apostle who wrote the Gospel and the letters, although we cannot be sure.

When? Probably around AD 95.

What's in it? Specific instructions to persecuted churches in Asia Minor (modern Turkey) in the form of letters, and an assurance that God is in control of world history and is moving it towards his own final goal.

Where does it fit? Shows us where God's plan is finally headed – to completely restore all things through the death and resurrection of Jesus, in whom death and sin have been conquered, making way for a new world, free from all the effects of human rebellion.

Continuing the journey...

What might all this mean for us? If we are right in the view that God makes himself known to us in Jesus and reveals Jesus to us in the Bible, then getting to know the Bible is one of the most important things that we can do.

This book has concentrated on how the Bible fits together; most of the time we have been thinking and analysing. Once we start to look more closely at what it says, we will find that our imagination and our emotions come into play. We will find that we want to worship God, that we are challenged about the need to change how we behave, and that we are given strength. The Bible is given to us not as just an object to engage our minds, but above all else, as God's word to us to make us what he want us to be. We read it so that we might meet with God, know him better and live for him. That is what makes the journey so exciting. Having seen something of the big picture what better than to explore some of the new places we have had a glimpse of in more detail. Just as looking at the globe can arouse a longing to travel and discover new places, so our look at the big picture should arouse a longing to explore more deeply.

In the geographical landscape there is variety: we can choose to lie beside a quiet stream in summer, listening to the trickling of the water and the murmuring of the bees; we can climb the peaks, the wind in our face to enjoy the exhilarating view from the summit, returning exhausted but satisfied at the end of the day to a hearty meal in the company of good friends; we can travel worn paths or break out in new directions. In our exploration of the Bible, we can enjoy the comforting words of some Psalms, be carried along with the challenge of the prophets to live justly, struggle to our profit with the complex thoughts of Paul.

This can take a range of forms. Some people try to read the Bible from beginning to end – well worth doing but challenging. Others follow some scheme of daily reading – recommended for all, but not everyone can work with a daily pattern. Another way is to read large chunks on a weekly basis.

Whatever way we choose, there is a lot to be said for the detailed exploration that enables us to hear from God. Here's to the continuing journey of exploration and discovery...

Taking it further

I hope that having come this far you'll want to continue the journey. There are many ways of doing that but here are a few suggestions.

Other ways of looking at the big picture...

God's Big Picture, Vaughan Roberts, IVP, 2003. The theme of God's kingdom as the theme of Scripture.

The Hitchhiker's Guide to the Bible, Colin Sinclair, Lion Hudson, 2008. A helicopter view of the Bible looking at each book.

The Big Story, Nick Page, Authentic Lifestyle, 2007. A light-hearted and helpful overview of the story of the Bible.

These three are longer and more challenging:

According to Plan, Graeme Goldsworthy, IVP, 2002.

The Drama of Scripture, Craig G Bartholomew and Michael W Goheen, SPCK, 2006.

The Mission of God, Chris Wright, IVP, 2006.

Digging into the background

A Bible handbook is an excellent way of finding out the details about people, customs and other things that will help to understand the Bible. One of the best starting points is the *The Lion Handbook to the Bible* (Lion Hudson, 2002). For more detailed study try *The New Bible Dictionary* (IVP, 1996). For an idea of where places are, the maps in the backs of many Bibles are a good starting point. For more detail, the *New Bible Atlas* (IVP, 1985) or the *Oxford Bible Atlas* (Oxford University Press, 1962) are my favourites.

Getting into the Bible

There are no shortcuts, and if we really want to know the Bible we have to put time and effort into reading it on a regular basis.

If you'd like to explore the Bible with others, *Christian Life and the Bible* (Conrad Gempf, Scripture Union/LBC Productions, 2006) is an exciting resource with DVD and interactive sessions. Or, if you'd prefer an online resource, take a look at Scripture Union's WordLive (www.wordlive.org) – details on the next page.

For details of different schemes – for individual and group use – both in print and on the internet, contact Scripture Union. Phone: 01908 856000 Web: www.scriptureunion.org.uk

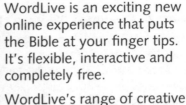
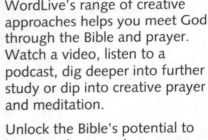